Maggid:
A Journal of Jewish Literature
I

Maggid

A JOURNAL OF **JEWISH LITERATURE**

EDITOR:
Michael P. Kramer

MANAGING EDITOR:
Deborah Meghnagi

ASSOCIATE EDITOR:
Shaindy Rudoff

PUBLISHER:
The Toby Press LLC

CONSULTING EDITORS:
Allen Hoffman

Linda Zisquit

CORRESPONDENCE:
For editorial, submissions &
books for review consideration:

Maggid
POB 8720, Jerusalem,
91086, Israel

or

Maggid
POB 8531, New Milford,
CT 06776-8531

editorial queries only can be
sent to maggid@tobypress.com

FOR SALES & SUBSCRIPTIONS:

The Toby Press LLC
POB 8531, New Milford,
CT 06776-8531

Submissions for future
issues: Maggid will consider

submissions of poetry,
prose, essays, and other
forms of Jewish literature.
All submissions must be
accompanied by an S.A.E. or
for overseas submissions, an
international reply mail coupon.
No e-mail submissions will be
accepted.

Vol 1, 2005
ISBN 1 59264 089 3

A CIP catalogue record for this
title is available from the British
Library

Typeset in Garamond by
Jerusalem Typesetting

Printed and bound in the
United States by
Thomson-Shore Inc., Michigan

Contents

INTRODUCTORIES

The Editors, Jewish American Writing:
350 New Years Later 1

Michael P. Kramer, Voices: An American Gothic
Tale; or, My Life With Jewish Literature 5

I. CREATIVE TEXTS, JEWISH CONTEXTS

A Note From the Editors 19

Allen Hoffman, From the Herring to the Leviathan 21

Rebecca Goldstein, The Two Cultures 31

II. FICTIONS

Cynthia Ozick, Refugees 45

Leslie Epstein, Ethiopia: A Prologue 65

Melvin Jules Bukiet, Return to Manhattan 71

III. VERSE

Shirley Kaufman, Circle 87

iii

Linda Zisquit, K'desha and Other Poems *91*

Mark Rudman, Inside The Park: Lines
on the Death of Billy Martin *97*

IV. FICTIONS

Max Apple, House of the Lowered: A Short Story *107*

Steve Stern, The Ice Sage *119*

Aryeh Lev Stollman, Bring Me into Paradise *135*

V. VERSE

Gerald Stern, L'chaim and Other Poems *149*

Rachel Tzvia Back, On Methods of
Concealment (A Manual) *155*

Alan Shapiro, Three Poems *159*

Alicia Ostriker, Tearing the Poem Up and Eating It *163*

Rachel Zucker, Graven Image Envy and Four Poems *169*

VI. ARCHIVES

Emma Lazarus, The Eleventh Hour *175*

VII. ON WRITERS AND WRITING

Joseph Skibell, Willis Alan Ramsey *&* Me:
A Bad Case of Second Novelitis *209*

Shaindy Rudoff, An Interview with Nava Semel *219*

Nava Semel, The Island of Israel *229*

Paul Zakrzewski, First Loves And Other
Sorrows: *First Loves,* by Ted Solotaroff *235*

Marshall E. Wilen, Out of Place: *The Place Will
Comfort You,* by Naama Goldstein *241*

CODA

Robert Pinsky, The Six-Pointed Star *249*

Introductories

The Editors

Jewish American Writing: 350 New Years Later

ROSH HASHANA 5415. Twenty-three Jews, give or take, settle in New Amsterdam. But that's putting it too emphatically. More precisely, they settle *for* New Amsterdam. They would have preferred, certainly, to stay in the prosperous Dutch colony of Recife, where Jews had lived comfortably for more than 20 years. But the Portuguese had returned to expel the Dutch who had expelled them a quarter century earlier, and the Dutch, including Recife's 600 Jews, went down to the sea in ships. They had intended to settle elsewhere, most to return to old Amsterdam, to be with family and friends, to get back on their financial feet. But one of the sixteen ships that left Recife did not arrive at its original destination. Somewhere on the Spanish Main it was raided by pirates, and its Jewish passengers—twenty-three men, women, and children—were compelled to change their plans. With the little they had left, the Jews contracted with the privateer Jacques de la Motthe for safe passage to the Jew-less Dutch colony of New Amsterdam, with its Jew-hating Calvinist governor, Peter Stuyvesant. It can't have been much of a Rosh Hashana. (Did they blow the *shofar*? Did they dip apples in honey? Did they search their souls?) They were Jews and they were now indigent. (Which did Stuyvesant hate more?) The governor immediately jailed a few for failing to pay their full passage and moved to rid himself of the rest. Still, the unwelcome newcomers knew about the influential Jewish lobby at the Dutch West India Company back in Holland. The Jews petitioned, and Stuyvesant was forced to let them stay.

What is it about those twenty-three Jews that now demands our attention? What is the narrative thread that links us to them? Did they provide us with a Jewish American Romulus? An Aeneas? Were they Conquistadores? Or Pilgrims? No, these Jews were not adventurers or dreamers. They did not come to New Amsterdam with a vision of a new promised land, of a kingdom of God on Earth. They were practical people, and they came reluctantly. They formed a congregation and built a cemetery. When we think of Jewish American culture, we do not think of them. Their Sephardi culture and institutions were overshadowed by those of the later German immigrants, as theirs were overwhelmed by those of the huddled East European masses who followed. They lived in Lower Manhattan, but they had no Lower East Side. No Statue of Liberty. No *shmatte* business. No sweat shops. No Workmen's Circle. No Educational Alliance. No Garden Cafeteria. No Hester Street. They had no Yiddish. They had no English. No vaudeville. No Tin Pan Alley. No Borscht Belt. No Broadway, no Hollywood. No Al Jolsen. No Eddie Cantor. No George and Ira Gershwin. No City College. No *Commentary*. No *Partisan Review*. No Bellow, no Malamud, no Roth. No Abraham Joshua Heschel. No Joseph B. Soloveitchik. No Holocaust, no Israel. No Sandy Koufax, no Bob Dylan. No flight to the suburbs. No Jewish Community Centers. (No shuls. No pools.) No summer camps for the kids. No bagels, no lox! True, those Dutch Jews had their heroes. One of their number once refused to show up in court on the Sabbath. Another became a licensed butcher, and would not slaughter swine. Ah, had their also been a poet among them!

ROSH HASHANAH 5765. *Maggid: A Journal of Jewish Literature* is launched. Our first issue celebrates this curious American anniversary. 350 years after that unanticipated and uncertain event, Jewish American writing has never been stronger, richer, more diverse. We chuckle at Irving Howe's glib prediction, a quarter century ago, of its imminent demise. A new generation of Jewish writers energetically ply their trade, while an older generation of writers, their eyes undimmed and their force unabated, continue to produce masterworks. It's been some time since American Jews had to fight for their rights, and since Jewish American writers have had to ignore or renounce their Jewishness in order to attract a mainstream audience. To be sure, some still bristle at being labeled Jewish writers, but, truth be told, never since those early settlers penned their petition to the Dutch West India Company have Jewish writers in America been so unencumbered by the albatross of particularity or have they so enthusiastically and rigorously mined Jewish resources for the purposes of art. Never before have they negotiated their two cultures so well. They find Jewishness everywhere. In this inaugural volume alone, they find it in the Bible and the Talmud and the Star of David, to be sure, but also in Karaism. They find it in midrash, and in a mother's disapproving glance. In herring and Haile Selassie. In frozen rabbis and graven images. They are haunted by the Holocaust and dream of paradise. They lament the death of Yitzhak Rabin and drink a gruff *l'chaim* to the disparate details of everyday life. Still, America is theirs, too. All theirs. St. Louis, Houston, Atlanta, Buffalo, Albany, and, of course, Manhattan. Hawthorne is theirs, and Huck Finn is theirs. Billy Martin and Willis Alan Ramsay. The Battle of the Bulge and 9/11. Auto supply stores, chain link fences, and red bud leaves. America is theirs even when they are no longer America's. Emigrant writers pack in their suitcases everything they can of America, and Israeli children and grandchildren wonder about their American roots, about life in the new/old world.

We launch *Maggid* with some of the same impulses with which we turn to those twenty-three Jews of New Amsterdam—not so much with a sense of mission or in search of meaning, but in celebration of the enigmatic but undeniable power of origins. And in hope of being surprised at the places Jewish imaginations take us, even to the point of wondering what a Jewish imagination might be.

Imagine that there had been a swashbuckler among those twenty-three Jews to fend off the fateful pirate attack that diverted them to America 350 years ago. What stories would we be telling today?

Michael P. Kramer

Voices: An American Gothic Tale; or, My Life With Jewish Literature

> *Rabbi Joshua says, "Give no heed to voices."*
> *—Babylonian Talmud*

It's 1965. I am a pubescent yeshiva boy in Crown Heights, Brooklyn, and I have begun to awaken to the possibilities of the wider world around me—to girls, of course, but also to music, and to literature. It's morning, the "Jewish" half of our school day. I am sitting in class, listening (more or less, for I notice out the window that the girls have gone out to recess) to one of the many ethical harangues of my rabbi, a *mussar shmuze* about proper behavior on shabbos. The rabbi is telling us that, besides prayer and family meals, we should spend the holy day in appropriate activities, not playing games with our friends (not even games technically permitted on the Sabbath), and not doing homework (for that would be preparing on the sacred Sabbath for the profane week), and not even reading secular books for pleasure. Certainly not socializing with girls. Rather, we should spend our time studying Torah.

I turn my gaze from the window, raise my hand, and naively ask what I think is a fair, and fairly harmless question: "What about *Jewish* literature? Can we read *Jewish* literature on shabbos?"

The rabbi's response is quick and unequivocal: "*Jewish* literature? *Jewish* literature? You mean Bellow and Singer? You mean *Roth*! That's not Jewish literature. The Mishnah, the Gemara, the Midrash—*that's* Jewish literature!"

This rabbi is a man of substance, youngish, tall, burly, unmistakably virile, with eyes that are alternately, and sometimes simultaneously, piercing and mild. When he had walked into class on the first day of the school year, he moved slowly, surveying us hormone-besotted boys with those eyes, calling us to attention. He took off his black hat and his black jacket, placing them neatly on a hook beside the blackboard. He sat down, stroked his beard dramatically, and opened his briefcase, very deliberately placing three items on the desk: a roll book, a gemara, and an iron spike. Without a word, his eyes continuing to survey the class, he took the spike in his hands, bent it with only the slightest hint of effort, and replaced it on the desk. Somebody gasped. He had our attention. He had our respect. His piety was proud and passionate, and his passion was persuasive. When he explained the Talmudic niceties of pecuniary responsibility when one man's ox gores another's, we felt the full force of the pounding steers. And when he told us what we were and were not allowed to do on shabbos, he threw the full weight of his powerful personality into it. No doubt about it, his word was law.

Now, as he shoots his sharp answer through my mostly innocent question, I feel mortified, angry and humbled. I certainly didn't mean to profane the sacred. To my childish mind, ethnic pride partakes of religious devotion. After Yom Kippur 1965, the solemn opening of the holy ark at *Kol Nidre* was inseparable from the mystifying, unhittable arc of Sandy Koufax's curve ball. So didn't the fact that it was *Jewish* literature—that it was written by Jews and about Jews—make it a little bit holy? Bellow's *Herzog* had just won the National Book Award, but, honestly, I'm not even sure that I knew then who Bellow and Singer were. It was, I would later learn, about a decade since Jewish writers had been thrust from the ethnic margins to the American mainstream, and they were still very much in fashion. But I was not a particular devotee of Jewish writers, neither on shabbos nor on weekdays. I do remember devouring an old, orange-covered copy of Mike Gold's *Jews Without Money* found by chance on my older sister's bookshelf—its opening chapter on Lower East Side prostitutes was irresistible—and our seventh grade English teacher had us read Bel Kaufman's *Up the Down Staircase* (Kaufman, the granddaughter of Sholem Aleichem, was purportedly a friend of his), but I imagine that I probably had something more like Harry Kemelman's *Friday the Rabbi Slept Late* in mind when I asked my question. Professor Moses Herzog, intellectual and neurotic, could not compete with Rabbi David Small, talmudist and detective. Okay, he wasn't an *Orthodox* rabbi, but he was still a Jew, a Jew who solved mysteries the goyim couldn't. A proud and admirable Jew, like Sandy Koufax.

My classmates laugh nervously. It is a traumatic moment in my life, and a formative moment in my intellectual development. As through a glass darkly, reluctantly, I begin to discern the difference between Judaism and Jewishness, between creed and culture.

The effects were profound and enduring, if often ironic. Years later, when, Talmud in hand, I enrolled at Columbia and began to study literature seriously, to become a scholar and critic, the voice returned to haunt me. "Jewish literature! Jewish literature!" As a result, I avoided Jewish literature like the plague. I was drawn at first to Shakespeare and the Elizabethans, and then to the Romantic poets, and then, inspired by a brilliant and charismatic professor (need I mention he was Jewish?) I turned my attention to early American literature, from the New England Puritans to Melville, Poe, and especially Hawthorne. I did my dissertation on Hawthorne and some obscure American philosophers of language. Goyim all, thank God. My earliest publications were on Puritan ministers, for which I immersed myself in Calvinist theology, on justification by faith, on the morphology of conversion, on visible sanctity, on the true sight of sin. With Cotton Mather's *Magnalia Christi Americana* I felt comfortable and safe; with Jonathan Edwards' *Sinners in the Hands of an Angry God*, I felt at peace. But not with Bellow's *Herzog*. Puritan literature was kosher. *Jewish* literature was *treif*.

⅌

Alas, I did eventually turn my attention to Jewish literature, shamed into it by a non-Jewish scholar who buttonholed me in the corridors of Hamilton Hall, assuming that, of course, I knew everything there was to know about Abraham Cahan and Mary Antin—not to mention Bellow, Malamud, and Roth. I was too embarrassed to admit that I knew nothing about them, or to explain why. So, like Goodman Brown, I ventured into the forest. I began to read, and the rabbi's voice began to haunt me again. "Jewish literature! Jewish literature!" It became particularly piercing when reading assimilationist narratives such as Antin's *The Promised Land*. And you can imagine what it sounded like when I read *Portnoy's Complaint*. (Okay, okay. *Re*-read.) But I persevered and made a very interesting discovery.

I discovered what anybody who knew anything about the field already knew, that the Jewish American writers of the mid-20th century—the most celebrated writers of the Jewish American Renaissance, the breakthrough writers whose success gave the field its *raison d'être*—these writers did not like to think of themselves as Jewish writers. Saul Bellow, for instance, was particularly uneasy about the claim. He took it as an insult. Not that he denied or belittled either cultural differences or the fact of his Jewishness. He claimed he was painfully conscious of what it meant to be a Jew in the twentieth century. Still, he refused to accept ethnicity as a sufficient definition of himself as a writer. He told interviewer after interviewer, who invariably felt compelled to ask the question, that he did not feel comfortable being pigeonholed in the "Jewish writer" category. Though he often wrote *about* Jews, he maintained that he did not write *as* a Jew, at least not on purpose. And as for the murky realm of the unconscious, well, this was possible, but surely only partial. After all, he *was* a Jew—but he was also a man, a mid-westerner, a hockey-fan, and so on. These were the multiple, complicated facts of his life, and, like any writer, he mined them with gusto, unapologetically. But he argued adamantly that, nevertheless, these facts did not define him. And they did not determine what he wrote.

It seemed that the more summarily Bellow rejected the "Jewish writer" label, the more the scholars, interviewers, and community leaders who idolized him smugly insisted he was just joking. But to me it was clear that Bellow wasn't joking. He suspected that the American Jewish community was trying to enlist him in its cause, to usurp his authority over his own writing, and he stubbornly resisted the attempt. He categorically refused to sacrifice artistic freedom and integrity in the name of public relations, no matter how noble the cause. In "The Writer as Moralist," an article he published in the *Atlantic Monthly* in 1963, he reasoned that a novelist could not truly be a writer and a propagandist at the same time. He could not begin with an explicit political purpose—even a wholly laudable one—and remain faithful to his art. "If a novelist is going to affirm anything," he then wrote, "he must be prepared to prove his case in close detail, reconcile it with hard facts." And since "facts are stubborn and refractory," the dedicated writer "must even be prepared for the humiliation of discovering that he may have to affirm something different." In other words, for Bellow, "the art of the novel itself has a tendency to oppose the conscious or ideological purposes of the writer, occasionally ruining the most constructive intentions." If being a Jewish writer meant to write *for* the Jewish community, or to please the Jewish community, even to express his Jewishness—then "Jewish writer" was a contradiction in terms. A *true* writer, committed to his art, could not, *by definition*, be a *Jewish* writer. He must simply be a writer. He cannot be defined or delimited by his roots, whatever they may be. Every *real* writer is, by definition, deracinated.

Not to be a Jewish writer was, for Bellow, not peevishness or playfulness but a matter of principle. Others could dismiss Bellow's protests. Maybe they needed to. But I took him at his word, and it sent shivers down my spine. His argument echoed inside me with uncanny familiarity. "Jewish literature! Jewish literature!" After all these years, the secret was revealed—Saul Bellow agreed with my rabbi! *Neither* of them thought that Bellow was a Jewish writer. For very different reasons, of course. My rabbi looked askance at all writing outside certain normative parameters, that exceeded or transgressed certain prescribed and delimited borders. If it was not Torah, it was not Jewish, by definition. Bellow and company looked suspiciously at all writing *within* normative parameters, that did not exceed or transgress, that did not claim autonomy. If it were bound by Torah or anything else, it wasn't literature—again, by definition. I imagined the two of them, rabbi and writer, sitting in a cafe somewhere in mid-town Manhattan, enjoying a good laugh at the expense of Young Goodman Kramer. "Jewish literature," Bellow quipped. "Jewish literature!" my rabbi snorted. Twin voices now followed me wherever I went, mocking me, letting me in on a cosmic truth I was not ready to hear.

Then one day, in a fit of inexpressibly sweet calmness (was I reading Edwards at the time?) it occurred to me that both were indeed right, that Jewish literature really did not exist at all. All those interviewers, all those scholars and critics, decades of eager, fawning, ordinary readers—they made it up. Jewish literature was nothing but a figment of their overheated and overzealous imaginations. For better or for worse, Jewish literature was, well, *just* literature—no more no less. *Augie March* was neither more nor less harmful to me than *Huckleberry Finn*. If I was going to hell, then I'd go to hell. It was a breakthrough. I saw the sunlight through the thicket. I left the forest. The voices fell silent.

᠅

Again, only for a while. My revelation eventually lost its luster, and I returned like a dog to its vomit. Who was I kidding? Didn't the same Bellow who was so vehement in his rejection of the Jewish writer category edit a book called *Great Jewish Short Stories*—and this in 1963, the same year he wrote that article about writers and morality and freedom in the *Atlantic*? Soon, too, I began to suspect the quickness of my spike-bending rabbi's rejoinder. What was he getting so worked up about? How did he even know about Bellow or Singer…or Roth? "Methinks," I thought, "they protest too much." Perhaps Jewish literature wasn't an illusion after all. Perhaps all the denials were devilish diversions, designed to distract me, to keep me off the scent. They were playing with me after all, though not in the way I thought. But why?

I am no David Small, but I've done a bit of research and I began to investigate. I discovered that, historically speaking, "Jewish literature" emerged as a category in Germany in the early part of the nineteenth century, pushed onto the stage of history by a confluence of social and ideological forces both from within and without Jewish communities: Enlightenment, Emancipation, Nationalism, Racialism, Romanticism, Anti-semitism. It was a heady, harrowing time, when Jews were readying themselves to shuck off their second-class status and head out of the ghetto on the promising but uncertain road to modernity. Some rushed out, seduced by sameness. Others held back, determined to remain different. Still others peered out cautiously, looking to see if there was not perhaps a middle road out of the ghetto. At the same time, the gentiles looked on: some with benevolence, some with amused indifference, some with fear and loathing. You might say that Jews were caught then between assimilation and anti-semitism: between, on the one hand, the desire to be like the goyim and, on the other hand, the insistence of many gentiles that they were not—and could never be. Or, if you prefer a more Gothic metaphor, they were bound on a rack of ambivalence, pulled this way and that, between apostasy and belief, reform and tradition, wanting to obliterate difference and preserve difference at the same time.

Snooping around the stacks, I discovered that "Jewish literature" emerged as a mode of mediation in this time of crisis and change. This was the golden age of national literary histories: of Johann Gottfried von Herder, of August and Friedrich von Schlegel, of Simonde de Sismondi, of Hippolyte Taine. A national literature, it was believed, was the product and sign of national greatness, the embodiment of its genius, of its *Volksgeist*. And the Jews—well, many said, you could hardly call them a nation. Everyone knew they had no literature. Okay, there was the Bible, but even Herder, the cultural relativist who had extolled the literary greatness of the Bible in *The Spirit of Hebrew Poetry*—even the eminent Herder believed that Jewish literary creativity went into decline with the destruction of the Temple and the Jews' subsequent exile. With the coming of Christianity, Judaism was superceded and the Jewish spirit went into permanent decline. Proof positive: the Talmud. My rabbi's Talmud, *My* Talmud.

Such a charge was tough to take. Jewish literary study—and I'm referring of course to the *Wissenschaft des Judentuums*, the forerunner of contemporary Jewish Studies—allowed Jewish scholars and their audience to thumb their noses at those who would look down their noses at Jews. We do indeed have a literature, the scholars cried, and we are able to stand shoulder to shoulder with the other civilized nations of the world. The literary historian Gustav Karpeles, student of the great Zunz himself, reported that, over the course of the nineteenth century, "the most valuable treasures of Jewish literature, a veritable Hebrew Pompeii, was unearthed from the mould and rubbish of the libraries." And though in some circles, he noted, "Jewish literature was still looked upon as the Cinderella of the world's literatures"—Cinderella, that is, *before* the ball—he could nevertheless offer his readers a detailed, "bird's eye view of the whole course of our literature," looking forward to the day "when justice will be done, Cinderella's claim be acknowledged equal to that of her royal sisters, and together they will enter the spacious halls of the magnificent palace of literature."

A fairy tale ending? Not exactly. The *Wissenschaft* enterprise was not simply a matter of dusting off literary relics and replacing them on the community mantle. Part and parcel of proving the existence of Jewish literature was making a case for Jewish writing *as* literature, a task that entailed the scholars' wresting control of Jewish writings from orthodox rabbis and setting themselves up as arbiters of Jewish cultural transmission. Changing Christian minds about the Jews entailed changing Jewish minds as well. Not all the *Wissenschaft* scholars went as far as Moritz Steinschneider, who is reported to have declared his final goal, "to give Judaism a decent burial." But for Jewish literary history to emerge, Judaism had to be reconceived.

This is what happened: God was benched to make way for the Jewish people—and Koufax began to warm up in the bullpen. The Talmud was resuscitated, not as holy text (fit for shabbos reading) but as *literature*. And the category of Jewish literature was expanded. No longer limited to the traditional Jew's halachic, midrashic, liturgical and homiletic texts (my rabbi's dream) but expanded to include all writing by Jews—orthodox and heterodox, religious and secular—Jewish literature could comprehend figures as different as Rashi the revered exegete, Maimonides the halachist and theologian,

Spinoza the heretic philosopher, and Heine the apostate poet. (We might even say that the purpose of Jewish literary history was to invent a tradition for writers such as Spinoza and Heine.) Each was a Jewish *writer*, none with more authority than another; each produced Jewish *literature*, none more authentic than another. The criterion for determining Jewishness was not religion (traditionally construed as a body of laws and practices) but, following Herder, the Jewish *Volksgeist*, the national spirit of the Jews, their racial essence, of which the Jewish religion was one, but only one, expression. And this was not all. The *Volksgeist* made each Jewish writer a *Jewish* writer, the emphasis squarely on the modifier. For all works produced by Jews, Gustav Karpeles wrote, "constitute only one class," as they all "are infused with the spirit of Judaism, and subordinate themselves to its demands." The Jewish spirit! Jewish writers, Jewish readers, Jewish literature—all held together in an inescapable, narcissistic embrace. A tantalizing *ménage à trois*.

So this is what exercised my rabbi so. This is what Bellow was *kvetching* about. As originally conceived nearly two centuries ago, Jewish literature represented a serious, substantive threat to what they believed in—to the authority of halachah on one hand, to the autonomy of the individual writer on the other. And how hard was it to get from *Volksgeist* to ethnicity? The voices returned, but wraith-like and plaintive now, as if begging me for help. "Jewish literature! Jewish literature!" Then one evening, while I was reading a volume of Hawthorne's short stories, the voices faded away, only to be replaced by other voices, a faint commotion at first, but growing steadily louder and closer, louder and closer, until I thought I could discern in the discordant din a familiar, chant-like rhythm. I rose and went to the window. It was a mob of boisterous voices, streaming towards me on a moonlit, midnight street. Men, women, and children in a confusion of costumes from what seemed to be different places and times, professionals and storekeepers, teachers and students, traveling salesmen and laborers, rabbis and radicals, from Lomze and London, Aleppo and Antwerp, pumping their fists in the air, shouting, "Jewish literature! Jewish literature!" In the midst of the mob, in an elegant, open carriage, was Gustav Karpeles himself, sitting in Germanic dignity, a mousy-looking coachman at the reins and a radiant young woman in glass slippers by his side, turning towards me, casting a look of derision and pity. Behind them sat two other figures, pale as death in the moonlight. One was young with a black beard; the other, elderly with steel-blue eyes. It seemed to me that their lips were moving, but I couldn't hear what they were saying. Both had looks of overwhelming weariness, pain, and humiliation, but the mob seemed wholly oblivious of their suffering. In fact, they seemed to be celebrating them, urging them to join in the chant. Above the mob, on a veranda overlooking the street, with shrewd eyes, winsome smile, a glass of wine in his hand, stood my publisher, Matthew Miller!

❧

The telephone rang, and Hawthorne fell to the floor. The voice on the phone was Matthew's. "Michael, did I wake you? Just wanted to know if *Maggid* was ready to go to press."

"I'm not sure I can go through with this," I said.

"Sure you can," he said kindly. "Do you need a few more days?"

"No, really," I protested. "I'm hearing voices," I wanted to say. "They're driving me mad! I can't take it any more." But I settled for, "Who wants a journal of Jewish literature anyway?"

"You do," he answered.

He was right, of course. I did. And so did everyone to whom I mentioned the idea. So what if I'm hearing voices. Is that necessarily such a bad thing? Maybe it's a good thing. Haven't Jews always been hearing voices? There were the prophets, of course, but I am hardly a prophet. I mean the voices that the Rabbis tell us about. Like the one that intervened in the dispute between Rabbi Eliezer and Rabbi Joshua concerning the oven of Akhnai. Convinced that his opinion, rejected by the other rabbis, was indeed correct, Rabbi Eliezer conjured up a number of supernatural signs—a tree uprooted itself, a river flowed backwards, the walls of the house of study began to collapse—an impressive show, but not enough to convince anyone. Then a voice echoed, declaring unequivocally, "Why do you dispute with Rabbi Eliezer, when his views are correct in all matters?" All eyes turn to Rabbi Joshua, who stood, unabashed, confident, and said, "This does not create in me a sense of obligation. The Torah tells us that cases are to be decided by a majority of judges, and that, as far as we should all be concerned, is the final word in the matter." Which no doubt led to Rabbi Joshua's dictum, quoted many times in the Talmud, "Give no heed to voices."

The first time I came upon that story must have been decades ago, probably about the same time I asked my spike-bending rabbi that fateful question. I sweated over it then. (That's another story.) But now it appeared to me in a wholly different light. Ben Bag-Bag says of the Torah, "Turn it, and turn it, for all is inside it." Well, I turned, and here was my answer. It was okay to hear the voices—Rabbi Joshua *heard* the voice, he didn't think it was some ventriloquist's trick—the key was simply not to heed them. In other words, listen, learn, just don't let them see you sweat.

There are other voices in Jewish tradition. There's the cautionary voice that speaks each and every day from Mount Sinai, declaring, "Woe unto mankind, for the effrontery shown the Torah." (Heard that one lately?) And there's the voice that spoke to and through the sixteenth-century halachist and mystic, Rabbi Joseph Karo, his personal *maggid* who rebuked him and encouraged him and revealed divine secrets to him. Nothing divine in the voices I hear, I'm sure of that—no doubt an indication of my unworthiness, but maybe as well, a sign of the times. Still, it's comforting to think of myself in the tradition.

I suppose it's also a sign of the times that I'm hearing not one *maggid* but many *maggidim*, each with a mind of his own. It's been difficult, as I've said. More than once I've found myself lifting my palms to my ears and shouting to one or another, "*Hak mir nisht keyn tsaynik, already!*" But, for the most part, I've learned to give each *maggid* his due.

"*Jewish literature!*" Gustav insists. "You're right," I concede, and go about editing the journal.

"*Jewish* literature?" Saul complains. "You're right," I admit, as I pick up the novel on my night table.

"Jewish *literature*?" my rabbi cautions. "You're right," I answer, trudging off at daybreak to my Talmud class.

"Give no heed to voices," Rabbi Joshua reminds me. I scratch my head and shrug my shoulders. "You're right!" What else can I say?

This is how it goes now, like an old joke. And now that I'm editing this journal I'm hearing more voices than ever. Contemporary voices of all kinds: brash and bashful, gruff and graceful, mad and mellow, sardonic and sentimental, wailing and whimsical. Deep, resonant voices and lilting, flute-like voices. Harsh voices that leave you red-faced, coy voices that keep you guessing. Charming voices and pedantic voices. Voices that echo other, older voices. Isn't that Jeremiah I hear? And over there, Judah Halevi? And that's Kafka, and that's Babel, and that's Sholem Aleichem. Wait a minute, that sounds just like Emily Dickinson! And is that Jonathan Edwards? And that sonorous voice, that's Melville, right? And that sly voice, that's Hawthorne. Ah, and how can you mistake Whitman! It gets a bit confusing sometimes, and often very loud. It's not easy, but I'm not complaining. I'm beginning to get the syncopation, to appreciate the peculiar harmonies. Each furnishes its part.

MICHAEL P. KRAMER *is the author of* Imagining Language in America *and editor of* New Essays on Bellow's Seize the Day, The Cambridge Companion to Jewish American Literature *(with Hana Wirth-Nesher) and Toby Press's edition of Hawthorne's* The Scarlet Letter *and* The House of the Seven Gables. *He teaches in the English Department at Bar Ilan University, where he directs the Anne Shachter-Smith Memorial Project in Literature.*

1. Creative Texts, Jewish Contexts

A Note From the Editors

In May 2003, the Bar Ilan University English Department held an international conference to inaugurate its new graduate program in creative writing. This English-language Masters program is the world's only "Jewish" one, offering students the opportunity to develop skills as they explore the relationship between their creative impulses and the contexts of Jewish and Israeli culture and experience. Hence its motto: "Creative Texts, Jewish Contexts." The program provides a place to mine, celebrate and argue about the use of Jewish material as a source of creativity, and offers a venue for thinking aloud about what the terms "Jewish writing" or "Israeli literature" might mean altogether. The program has already become an international magnet for writers and students. To date, approximately fifty writing students from the u.s., Israel, Canada, England, South Africa, Zimbabwe and India have entered our classrooms, taught and visited by writers such as Allen Hoffman, Melvin Jules Bukiet, Aharon Appelfeld, Eva Hoffman, Rebecca Goldstein, Alicia Ostriker, Aryeh Lev Stollman, Aida Nasrallah, Joseph Skibell, Linda Zisquit, Rachel Tzvia Back, Pearl Abraham, Steve Stern, Jane Bernstein, Bharati Mukherjee, Michal Govrin and Michael Oren—to name just a very few.

The two essays that follow were originally presented as talks at the 2003 inaugural conference—Allen Hoffman's at a panel called "Jewish Writing in English: The View from Here and There," and Rebecca Goldstein's at a panel entitled "The Jewish Mind and the Culture of Science." In the ways in which they grapple with questions of ethnic and creative identity and influence, and with the issue of how Israel has effected their sense of place, in the degree to which they hover between ambivalence and excitement, and between the scholarly and the imaginative, and perhaps most importantly, in the way that the arguments presented are ultimately outdone by the pleasures provided by the texts themselves, both essays capture the spirit of the conference, and of the program.

Allen Hoffman

From the Herring
to the Leviathan

A number of years ago, perhaps as many as fifteen, I was sitting in my studio in the Jewish Quarter of the Old City of Jerusalem and the phone rang. Joe Lowin, whom I hadn't met, was calling, and asked whether I would talk to him about my use of midrash in fiction. Joe was the first to refer to "writing in the midrashic mode" which I certainly do. Although I was quite confident about the midrashic component, I was, however, somewhat hesitant to respond because of the geographical component: I had moved to Jerusalem. F. Scott Fitzgerald said, "There are no second acts in American lives." I am not sure that he's altogether correct, but I would suggest that almost all Jewish lives are second acts. And what is more Jewish than a life in Jerusalem? Jerusalem is text and Jerusalem is context. Jerusalem, then, is even the midrash of itself. Joe, I am very pleased that you are here participating in our conference as I feel the time has come to respond to your inquiry.

The title of our conference "Creative Texts, Jewish Contexts" is also the name of our new graduate writing program. I coined it, and I find it liberating because it does not attempt to define what is a Jewish text or Jewish writing. I suspect that some of you may be interested in such a definition, and since I don't want anyone to go away disappointed for a further fifteen or so years, I shall tell you; for it does have something to do with midrash. Jewish writing is any text that leaves you reaching for a piece of herring. Note that this is a very inclusive definition: it presents no problem for those on salt-free or strict vegetarian diets. You don't have to eat the herring, you only have to reach for it. Since this might come as a surprise to some, it might be helpful to provide general parameters of Jewish literature: The greatest American Jewish novel is *Huckleberry Finn*; like the youthful Abraham, Huck recognized the truth and smashed the idols. The greatest midrash in the English language is *King Lear,* which is, of course, the midrash on Western man. The best of the assimilated Jewish authors is Tolstoy; in *War and Peace* he very cleverly disguises the Jewishness that provides the astonishing coherence of his tale. Literature is not all fun and games, so I feel obligated to mention the foremost halachist among modern writers, T.S. Eliot, who so aptly summed up the ultra-orthodox Lithuanian tradition, "The spirit killeth, but the letter letteth live."

The bottom line is that stories invite stories and this is especially true of the classical Jewish midrashic and talmudic tradition. The fundamental text is the Bible, the Torah, and the book of books is Genesis, and the story of stories is that of Creation. It is important to note that the Creation text is a story: it is not a manual or a cookbook of how God created the world. It is how God wants us to understand His creating the world. It may be true as true can be, but it remains a story. The midrash on creation tells us that God created the world by looking into the Torah. To say the least, this is a very rich midrash, but what I would like to have us focus on is that God explains to us that He created the world by studying the story by which He will tell us of His creating the world. The old conundrum: what came first—the verse or the midrash? Now, I am fully aware that some of you might wish to resolve this textual dilemma by moving into the Kabbalah, which teaches that the text of the Torah assumes different textual forms in differing cosmic periods. I reject making that move for at least three reasons: one, I detest Madonna and her music; two, I am not about to enter any groves, orchards, or forests as I have allergies, and only one of the four sages who entered the mystical orchard emerged unharmed. And three, whatever it is or is not, the kabbalah is not a literary tradition. In that sense, it is not our tradition. (It can be helpful in emergencies but even then at a significant risk: Kabbalists are like chiropractors; the good ones can work miracles but the bad ones can kill you and you never know which is which until it is too late.) Yes, "the letter giveth life." Stories invite stories. Stories beget stories.

If stories come from stories, where does man come from? According to the Biblical text, man is molded from the earth and God breathes life into him. The midrash suggests that God in His modesty turned to consult with the angels before creating man. The angels objected: man will be sexually licentious, adultery his specialty; God answered that if man were not sexually licentious, he would not people the earth. Man, the angels accused, will be a thief. And God answered them that, if he weren't, he would not earn a livelihood. The angels told the truth and so did God. Man is of the earth: man is of God. Man is always capable of sanctifying the name of God, creating beauty, art, music, even literature. Simultaneously, man is always a lewd bundle of protoplasm encasing a core of excrement. He has his good days and he has his bad days, his ups, his downs, his ins, his outs. What you see is what you get. And what you get remains to be seen.

Rabelais certainly learned in this *beis midrash* and I assume that he learned well because he wrote so well. For myself, and for anyone who so chooses, these sacred texts may be some of the classical proof texts that are Jewish contexts. Can it be a mitzvah to celebrate in fiction such a little mamzer as midrashic man, however sublime? In the words of the godless critic, where do we derive the authority to write creatively about midrashic man? I would suggest that the invitation to enter the creative dialogue in celebrating midrashic man occurs in the passages in Genesis in which God states that He cannot hide the destruction of Sodom from Abraham and informs him of the city's imminent destruction. In response, Abraham enters into that very dramatic, very specific, very insistent one-on-one bargaining with God over the number of righteous individuals that it would take to save the sinful city from annihilation. Abraham exhibits chutzpah that God indulges and even relishes. When the bear market in the righteous crashes from fifty to ten, God turns away and then Abraham "returns to his place" because he still can't cover the price. The midrash suggests that even though God has turned away, Abraham's "returning to his place" results in the destruction. I hesitate to the use the term "game-playing" in describing this fantastic haggling defense by midrashic man, of midrashic man, against the Creator of midrashic man. But, I suspect, game-playing it is—and our invitation to write. Not only is there a God, but also what is worse, He has a sense of humor.

What I have said until now, I could have told Joe on the phone lo those many years ago, especially as he was paying for the conversation. It is, of course, a mitzvah to call critics collect, but it isn't so easy to get them to accept the charges. They prefer to assess the charges.

No leviathan—certainly not the midrashic Leviathan of Creation and of Jerusalem which I shall soon be discussing—begins as a herring. In my case, however, such a leviathan began with a herring, and I do feel that they are familially related. As a kid I didn't like herring; I grew into liking it and developed a taste for Jewish literature as well—hence, our definition of Jewish literature. Back in the suburbs of St. Louis where I grew up, herring was a fact, a very Jewish fact, perhaps even a defining Jewish fact. It is our "soul" food. I never knew non-Jews to eat it; the menu in the Immigration Museum on Ellis Island decrees "Herring for the Hebrews." In any event, after the services, in our small, very plain Orthodox synagogue, the stalwart band of congregants would turn resoiutely to the kiddush table. Along with whiskey, crackers, and ei-kichelech—(a sort of horrendous, flaky dry Jewish biscuit that probably inspired untold numbers of Czarist hunger strikers not to end their self-inflicted tortures)—lay the reliable, faithful herring, a powerful but modest presence. The herring on the table seemed to have an awareness that it had gotten there by default. Culinarily, it was the lowest common denominator: It was kosher, it was inexpensive, and it kept—forever. In slices, it was more attractive, but even that virtue came by default because there was some something woefully lugubrious about the whole fish. When you looked at the entire fish, you knew that in its brine it could last forever, which was not the best advertisement for eternity. Unlike the mummified cats and dogs found in Egyptian tombs, creatures that seemed to have acquired through their preservation some recondite secret of the ages, the herring seemed merely to be rueing the unfortunate fact that it had been dropped into its reeking saline environment.

The older Jews, however, were very enthusiastic. My father, in spite of the fact that he was a very reasonable man, would rhapsodize over its presence. "Boys" he would declaim passionately, "you give a Jew a piece of herring and he's happy!" It certainly made them happy. The strangest ritual remark, one that was offered as a serious declaration and seemed to fly in the face of all briny reality, was offered by a very solid, respected gentleman, Nat Seltzer, owner of a successful chain of dry goods stores. Every Shabbos he would announce that the herring was fresh from the *mikveh*. When we asked, "How can you tell?" He answered definitively, "Look at it! Fresh from the *mikveh*." We children knew little about *mikveh*s, but we did know that there were no fish in the community ritualarium, much less dead, salted ones. Fresh did not seem to go with herring; the statement did mystify us. Other remarks seemed more understandable and attested to the herring's pedigree as soul food. One was the oft-told story of the Jew, riding on the train somewhere in Eastern Europe and quietly eating his herring, when a goy asked why Jews are so smart. The Jew pointed to the herring he was cutting. The goy asked to purchase some and the Jew sold him several pieces. After tasting a few pieces, the goy said, "You're charging me ten kopecks a piece and for ten kopecks I could buy a whole fish." "Ah!" the Jew announced, "You see, you're getting smarter already!" That was always warmly received. And there was the old proverb, "*be-mekom she-ain ish, iz a herring oich a fish!*" "In a situation where there is no real man, even a herring can pass for a fish!" Or, I suppose to capture some of the rhyming flavor, "In a place that lacks a man, even a herring goes into the pan." The proverb endorsed a populism that was close to our Midwestern hearts. Fighting Bob Lafollette might have carried Wisconsin with that slogan, as herring goes so very well with *milchigs* as well as *fleishigs*. It's not a big fish but one size fits all.

For a number of years, the herring lay undisturbed in its brine. Given the fifteen-year delay, it took some time to befriend the leviathan. Still, I was the first kid on my block to have one, but I had to move blocks, even continents to do so. It took some serious studying, learning, and living to get there. I had an advantage in that I swim well; never any fear of the *mikveh* and a certain stoic delight in doing laps in the *yam hatalmud*, the sea of the talmud, with an overt delight in splashing around in the imaginative midrashic passages. And eventually while learning how one legally acquires ownership of a boat in the tractate of *Baba Basra*, you turn the page—in any reasonable *beis midrash* this takes the better part of a lifetime—and there is the leviathan: the herring's big brother, the herring's grandfather, and the herring's successor.

The leviathan of creation, the grandfather fish, and the leviathan of the World To Come, the herring's successor, are very much midrashic creatures. The word "leviathan" does not appear at all in the Torah; indeed, it appears in Isaiah, Psalms, and the Book of Job. But the midrash on Genesis tells some tall fish stories; put your rubber waders on. In Genesis 1:21, on the fifth day, the midrash interprets "taninim gedolim" the "great sea monsters" or "huge creatures" as the leviathan. God creates a pair of leviathans but immediately realizes that the garage isn't big enough; if they were to multiply, they would destroy the world. After all, to err is divine so God makes amends by slaying the female and castrating the male. Not exactly an equal opportunity Destroyer, but by slaying the female, He provides an opening for feminist interpretation; and as for castrating the male, Freud "*vais.*" You win a few; you lose a few. Ecologically, there is a potential problem here but the Deity salts the flesh of the female leviathan for the banquet of the righteous in the World to Come: don't leave your seats, it's an invitation-only affair. While waiting for the affair to begin, God has to fill up his twelve-hour day, so three hours a day he studies Torah (naturally); three hours a day he judges the world; three hours a day, He sustains the world; and three hours a day He plays with the leviathan. A galaxy for a Frisbee, a black hole for a bone, a good time was had by all. Wait, a black hole for a bone? Well, it was a horrendously divine mistake. In Creation, the leviathans might have been voted cutest couple for they were also known as Samael and Lilith: the Kabbalistic Mr. and Mrs. Satan. And evil is as evil does; God frolics with him, no less. For those of you detest herring, you can claim that on the cosmic culinary menu of creation, the leviathan cannot be found among the appetizers unless theodicy is in column B. But there will be no problem with dessert. When the righteous receive their just desserts the recipe calls for the death of the male leviathan that signifies the disappearance of evil in Messianic times. Happy days are here again!

Note that the righteous—earlier the market had crashed on them—now sit around the table eating salted fish. Herring, you've come a long way, baby! And, note, that God made a mistake and he admitted it. And where does this take place? You bet—downtown! The extra fish is sold in the markets in Jerusalem and the skin of the leviathan is spread upon the walls of Jerusalem and from its hide radiates the divine light of Creation which has also been preserved for the righteous. See what happens when you follow the instructions? Not exactly an Italian restaurant with the checked tablecloth and dripping candle in the empty Chianti bottle; you'll have to adjust.

That's what can happen if you reach for the leviathan. There are three mitzvahs (commandments) that one performs with one's entire body: living in the land of Israel, dwelling in the *sukkah*, and immersing oneself in a *mikveh*. What these three share is uncommon exposure, both spiritual and physical. Spiritually, the *mikveh* provides total purification, the *sukkah* permits dwelling in the shade of the *shechinah*, the holy presence; and whereas these two are temporary, in the Holy Land one lives in the Palace of the King with a long-term lease. On the other hand, taken together, the physical exposure results in no oxygen, no clothing, no roof, no insulation, and in Israel—no Sunday, Knesset politics, Egged drivers, suicide bombers, etc. I'm not suggesting that we as Jews don't have any sense. There is a real mystery here. Given our history (Biblical, ancient, and modern) given our place in the world (southern Syria), given our place in the society of nations (or the lack thereof), why are we so optimistic about what should be done, what can be done, and what must be done?

In short, we are all messianists—every last depressive one of us. It is only a question of context: Moses, Marx, macrobiotics, just to name a few. For Jews the clock is always ticking—and it's always ticking redemption: *tikkun, tikkun, tikkun* constantly. Of course, what is not one's own brand is an anathema. In Israel, all the more so. Some resolutely press for the end in the settlements of Yehudah and Shomron; others hear the certain footsteps of the Messiah in the frozen streets of Oslo. I prefer literature. More precisely, I prefer literature in English. I always studied the classical Jewish texts in the original and I do so now in a Hebrew-speaking milieu. There I was a Jew; here I am an Anglo-Saxon—may Beowulf be remembered for a blessing! Alienation comes with the territory; I welcome it as a positive fact, and the writing is in English. Perhaps for our children it may be different. My wife and I insistently tell them that they have all the advantages that we never had: immigrant parents and poverty. Even reaching for the herring has its hazards. It's even trickier reaching for the leviathan with a herring in the other hand. That, too, is understandable; on the revolving carousel of Jewish life there are only second acts—especially if you reach for the brass ring on the walls of Jerusalem.

So we made aliyah to Jerusalem. For many years, I told friends that we had "backed into the future with great foresight" and that we were here "permanently for the time being." "Permanently for the time being" seemed apt, absurd, and even original until our new Bar Ilan graduate writing program described me as "the permanent writer-in-residence." That's Ramat Gan, for you, but I live in Jerusalem. And Jerusalem is text and midrash. In Psalm 122, the psalmist speaks of going up to Jerusalem in joy and standing resolutely within Jerusalem's gates. The third verse, *"k'ir shechubrah-lah yachdav,"* is very curious and speaks of Jerusalem as a city that is "very compact together" or, perhaps, "very connected together." The midrash interprets this as teaching that what is connected together are the two Jerusalems, the heavenly Jerusalem and the earthly Jerusalem. Very boldly, the midrash continues that God will not enter the heavenly Jerusalem until the Jews enter the earthly city. This endows each of us with great power and responsibility—even cosmic power and responsibility. (It's one thing for a sprawling family of "*frum*" ultra-Orthodox Jews to move in and ruin the neighborhood, but to ruin the universe!) And we have this incredible cosmic opportunity because of God's divine absence from heavenly Jerusalem; God, so to speak, is out to lunch. Or, as Huckleberry Finn might put it, "God has gone fishin'." In the mighty Mississippi, Huck might hook a supremely fine catfish worthy of the Duke of Bilgewater. A few hours downstream in St. Louis, Nat Seltzer might produce a herring fresh from the *mikveh*—worthy of a kiddush table. But the Jew who enters Jerusalem might discover one day that the Proprietor has returned with the show-stopping, prize-winning all-time catch from Creation, the leviathan! And wondrous as that may be, it should come as no surprise, because if all roads lead to Rome, which they surely do, all *mikveh*s flow to Jerusalem.

That's the view from here, Joe.

ALLEN HOFFMAN *grew up in St. Louis, Missouri, and currently lives in Jerusalem's Old City. He is the author of the award winning* Kagan's Superfecta and Other Stories *and three novels in the* Small Worlds *series:* Small Worlds, Big League Dreams, *and* Two For the Devil. *Currently he is completing the fourth volume,* Instruments of Desire. *He is a member of the English faculty and Permanent Writer-In-Residence in Bar Ilan University's graduate writing program.*

Rebecca Goldstein

The Two Cultures

I meant my title to be vague; I was deliberately cultivating obscurity—like a Frenchified philosopher. "The Two Cultures." Which two cultures?

The phrase itself famously comes from C.P. Snow, the writer/ scientist/politician of the World War II generation. In his 1959 Rede lecture, Snow dissected a pernicious intellectual trend that he detected and christened. The sciences and technology, on the one hand, he complained, and the arts and humanities on the other, had so diverged from one another as to all but halt significant communication and curiosity across the great divide. Scientists are illiterate. They couldn't even name the great books, much less lay claim to having read them. Worse, the artists and humanists (and Snow, as I remember, came down harder on this group than on the scientists), although living in an increasingly technological age, are shamelessly ignorant of how any of it works, of the scientific theories that lie behind it all. This lack of a common universe of discourse and interests impoverishes both sides, Snow implied, impoverishes the culture as a whole.

So there's that idea, the famous C.P. Snow idea of the two cultures. And maybe that's what I had in mind by my title.

But then, of course, this is a conference on writing, on poetry and fiction; and not just on any writing, but on Jewish writing, a celebration of the first program in the world devoted to Jewish writing, and this context suggests other interpretations of the phrase "the two cultures."

The very notion of Jewish writing, of the Jewish writer, might seem to point a finger, either approbatory or admonishing, at some ghostly fissure in a common culture, to raise up the suggestion of a latent bifurcation, to introduce, as Shaindy Rudoff put it in her thoughtful remarks opening this conference, "the problematics of 'ours'." The suggestion of cultural duality is, perhaps, why the very idea of Jewish writing, of the Jewish writer, makes many writers look quickly around for the nearest exit, including writers who have set the gold standard for Jewish-American writing, such as Saul Bellow, Philip Roth, Bernard Malamud, Cynthia Ozick, each of whom has emphatically rejected the designation of "Jewish writer." So there's that mildly controversial notion of the two cultures, the one that seems possibly to be lurking in the very idea of a Jewish writer, and one which raises questions uncomfortably relevant to this conference.

And then, of course, this isn't just a conference on Jewish writing, but a conference in Israel on Jewish writing, attended by both Israeli and American writers and scholars. This presents yet another possible interpretation of "the two cultures," viz. diasporic vs. Israeli culture. C.P. Snow had lamented that the scientists and humanists were becoming profoundly uninteresting to each other, unwilling to stretch their minds to take in the ever more alien experience of the other side. Are we, Israeli and Diaspora writers, possibly becoming uninteresting to one another, driven apart by our widening divergence of experience? Has Israel produced an entirely new kind of Jew, too unconnected with the historical forces that shaped our identities in *chutz la-aretz* to be grasped by the imaginations of *non-Israeli* Jewish writers? (Having spent a good part of this past weekend with my daughter on the beach at Tel Aviv, I'm inclined to take this possibility very seriously.)

So here are at least three possible interpretations of this phrase, "the two cultures," two of them of direct relevance to the context provided by this conference, one of them quite irrelevant, having nothing specifically to do with Jewish writers, many of them American, gathering in Israel. And it's of course to the quite irrelevant idea of the two cultures that I want to speak today, the one that appears to have nothing very much to do with the subject of writing and Jewish writers.

(Because I have, parenthetically, to confess, that every time I'm asked to speak on the topic of Jewish writing, as a Jewish writer, I find myself awkwardly dumbfounded. I was trained to be a philosopher of science, a profession to which I've recently returned. There are days when I have a hard time convincing myself that I've ever written fiction at all. And my being associated with Jewish writing, no matter how tangentially—though I see from the title of Emily Budick's talk that perhaps she'll explain how my connection isn't quite so tangential—but my being so associated, in whatever way, also never ceases to amaze me. I'll make a little confession. I've been trying to become a typical assimilated American Jew for just about my whole life. It's pathetic really, I'm just so bad at it. I've tried to use my hard-earned, rigorous education as a conduit away from the particularities of my background—from what one of my fictional characters once called the "accidents of precedents." The subjects that I studied, math and physics and philosophy, most especially philosophy, were subjects I wasn't supposed to study, given the accidents of my precedents, not as a girl, and especially not as an Orthodox Jewish girl. Especially not philosophy. I first learned a little bit about philosophy when I was a student in a right-wing, all-girls yeshiva. What I learned was that it was the *worst* thing that you could possibly study. It was in *historia*—Jewish history—and we were learning about that *apikorus* Benedictus Spinoza—who was born Baruch Spinoza. See what happens, little girls, when you think you're so smart and start questioning everything. (Was it my imagination that my teacher's smoldering eyes were fixed specifically on me?) From Baruch to Benedictus! The very word, *apikorus*, testifies to the deep suspicion with which our tradition regards philosophy. The word derives from the name of that famous Greek philosopher, Epicuras, who taught of the fundamental importance of pleasure in justifying our ends and also had such a horror of beans. The far more approving adjective and noun 'epicurean' is also derived from his name. But for the Jews, the Greek philosopher yielded the word for heretic—more on account of his pleasure-principle than his legume-phobia. When my mother learned that my oldest daughter was going to major at Harvard in philosophy, she offered her a tidy sum of money *not* to, saying "Look what it did to your mother." I loved these subjects, math and physics and philosophy, *especially* philosophy, not only for themselves alone—for their mind-bashing toughness that pushed you to the limits of your understanding and then a tiny bit beyond—but also for how far away from the accidents of my precedents they seemed to be carrying me. Grasping Plato's Forms, or Einstein's four-dimensional manifold, or Gödel's incompleteness theorem, it didn't matter a hoot who I was, whether girl or boy, Jewish or not, poor or rich. I called the object of my desire "objective knowledge" and the taste of it in my mind was of pure sweet water. I loved above everything the sense that I was reconstituting my mind, transforming the passive ideas that had been handed to me by the conditions of my birth into the active ideas I had derived simply through seeking rational explanations. I loved that all of us who so dedicated ourselves to this rational pursuit could end up with the same ideas; that, in a sense, we could end up with the same mind, the mind of objectivity itself—one approximating *Deus sive Natura*, as my beloved *apikorus* Spinoza put it. So my having on occasion written the sort of fiction that gets me invited to conferences such as this one, fiction that positively revels in the accidents of my very Jewish precedents, continues to surprise me. No matter how many times I retake it, I continually flunk out of Assimilation 101.)

Having now spent precious parenthetical minutes telling you what I don't want to talk about, let me talk a bit about what I do want to talk about: the two cultures of science and technology, on the one hand, and the arts and humanities, on the other. There's been something rather interesting going on, at least in the English-speaking world, the last few years. Not only have some scientists taken to writing quite literate and vivid accounts of their science, to which the public has responded in bestseller-making numbers—I'm thinking here of such publishing phenomena as Stephen Hawking's *A Brief History of Time* and Roger Penrose's *The Emperor's New Mind*. But also a sizable number of literary artists have dipped into the sciences for their subjects, characters, and inspiration.

There have been, just over the last five years, a remarkable number of plays and movies and novels that have devoted themselves to science, and not in the old Frankensteinian mold either, featuring the soulless scientist ruthlessly seeking a knowledge inimical to the well-being of humankind. Rather this new brace of works presents the scientific enterprise in sympathetic, in even heroic, terms.

There was, of course, the academy award winning *A Beautiful Mind*, presenting the Hollywood version (inspired by Sylvia Nasser's wonderful biography of the same name) of the strange sojourn through mathematics and madness of the Nobel-prize-winning John Nash, who incidentally *I* had named "the phantom of Fine Hall" in my first novel, *The Mind-Body Problem*. I've never gotten credit for that epithet, by which even *The New York Times* had called him at the time of his Nobel, and I want to use this occasion to get my due. When I'd written that novel Nash had been totally in his own world, but still I'd worried about dubbing him with this disparaging title and I'd actually consulted a psychiatrist and asked her what the odds were of his ever regaining his faculties. She told me, "Oh, it's practically zero." And then the epithet stuck, everyone called him "the phantom," and then he got better, and I was worried, but it seems that he *likes* the nickname, he calls himself "the phantom," so it's all OK.

Anyway, in addition to *A Beautiful Mind*, there was also the very fine movie *Pi*, featuring not just two brilliant mathematicians, mentor and disciple, but evil Wall Street types and Kabbalistic Jews. I recommend it. There was Michael Frayn's award-winning *Copenhagen*, again a great critical and popular success, a three-person drama featuring the quantum physicists, Niels Bohr and Werner Heisenberg, as well as Bohr's wife, Margrethe. The play (rather ponderously, I thought) uses Heisenberg's Uncertainty Principle as a metaphor for the uncertainty of ever ascertaining the true motives of human behavior, in this case, Heisenberg's motive in heading up the Nazi atomic bomb project. Was he trying, as argued by his apologists (among whom the playwright can be numbered), to sabotage it from within, or did he just get his arithmetic very wrong, grossly miscalculating the amount of enriched uranium that would be required to get a nuclear holocaust going? There was also, appearing briefly at Lincoln Center with Alan Alda in the lead role, the play QED, about the last days of the *sui generis* Richard Feynman (that's 'QED,' as in quantum electrical dynamics), and another longer-running play, *Proof*, a family drama that featured three mathematicians. I also caught a few smaller productions, such as an off-Broadway musical, *Star Gazers*, that had Galileo, Kepler, and Tycho Brahe singing and hoofing up a storm.

In fiction, as well, there has been some significant interest in the sciences, knowledgeable books that don't reduce scientists and mathematicians to the clueless automata that we'd seen before but instead offer much more layered, sympathetic portraits. More importantly, these works often demonstrate considerable grasp of some of the more subtle and exciting aspects of contemporary math and physics. I'm thinking particularly of the work of Richard Powers, many of whose books demonstrate scientific intimacy, the very celebrated *Einstein's Dreams*, by Alan Lightman, and the work, too, of my esteemed fellow panelist, Aryeh Lev Stollman. The very title of his last book, a wonderful collection of short stories, *The Dialogues of Time and Entropy*, indicates the presence of this artistic trend of drawing from the sciences.

What's going on here? Perhaps the rapprochement is partly a matter of the way in which technology has insinuated itself into the processes by which most—with the exception of a few holdout Luddites—humanists think and artists create. It's difficult to maintain the old image of the demonically soulless scientists, draining the beauty from the world in the course of explaining it, while gathering one's evidence from the internet. Snow had placed great emphasis on the fact that our culture is becoming ever more technological, and had asked how the artists and humanists could partake of this technology without its penetrating their thought processes. Well, maybe he was right and the penetration is happening before our eyes. And maybe with the penetration comes an attitudinal change, so that the scientific enterprise is no longer seen as inimical to the free human spirit, but rather as one of its most heroic expressions: the attempt to get outside ourselves, our ego-tainted worldviews, and take in the nature of the world at large, what Einstein called the out-yonder.

In the "Autobiographical Notes" that Einstein supplied with his typical self-mocking good humor for the *Festschrift* celebrating his 67th birthday compiled by Paul Arthur Schilpp, he explicitly identifies the scientific quest to reach out beyond the borders of one's own personality and experience in order to make contact with the not-oneself as the spiritual center of his life:

> "It is quite clear to me that the religious paradise of youth, which was thus lost, was a first attempt to free myself from the chains of the "merely personal," from an existence which is dominated by wishes, hopes, and primitive feelings. Out yonder there was this huge world, which exists independently of us human beings and which stands before us like a great eternal riddle, at least partially accessible to our inspection and thinking. The contemplation of this world beckoned like a liberation…. The mental grasp of this extra-personal world within the frame of the given possibilities swam as a highest aim half consciously and half unconsciously before my mind's eye…. The road to this paradise was not as comfortable and alluring as the road to the religious paradise; but it has proved itself as trustworthy, and I have never regretted having chosen it."

This is a deeply eloquent statement of Einstein's credo as a scientist; science as spiritual salvation, akin to religious salvation. It happens also to be a vivid elucidation of what Spinoza had called *amor intellectualis Dei*, the intellectual love of God, in Spinoza's ethics the highest form that our emotional/cognitive/spiritual development can take.

At other times, Einstein spoke about the role that beauty played in his life as a scientist. For example, when the philosopher of science, Hans Reichenbach, asked Einstein how he had felt when empirical evidence supporting his theory of relativity had finally been gathered—it had awaited a solar eclipse to see whether the gravitational pull of the sun would bend light rays as Einstein's theory predicted—Einstein had answered Reichenbach that he hadn't been so impressed with this empirical evidence as the rest of the world had. He had already known that the theory was true. It had to be true, he told Reichenbach, because it was so beautiful.

Fellow fiction writers and poets: does this ring a bell? It *has* to be true because it's so beautiful? How similar this sounds to our attempts as artists, as writers: this attempt to make our way out of the narrow precincts of our own personalities, to get beyond ourselves, hard as that may be, guided by our commitment to the forms of beauty.

Obviously, there is a great deal of diversity in human nature: who should know this better than we writers? The deep emotions motivating individual scientists and individual artists run the gamut (even in one and the same individual) from the Seussian "look at me! look at me! look at me now!" to Einstein's impersonal passion.

Einstein's confession of utter indifference to the mere empirical evidence for his theory, when beauty was on his side, is very impressive, or ought to be, I think, to us artists, hinting at the profound affinity between our "two cultures." There is some serious beauty to be found in the mathematical sciences: elegance and refinement and grandeur. And even if one's taste doesn't go in that direction, toward that extreme objectivity that tries to leave behind all traces of the human element, even if, as is often the case with us literary types, inhuman visions leave one distinctly cold, still it's good for us all to remember that deep down, at the deepest levels of their work, the scientists, too, are artists. Faced with two or more theories that are empirically adequate, the scientist will resort to aesthetic considerations—elegance, refinement, simplicity, grandeur—in deciding which theory offers the best explanation. All things being equal, the more beautiful theory is the scientifically better theory.

Artist, humanist, and scientist, each in his or her own way committed to an expansiveness in human experience, see themselves, I think, increasingly on the same side of a deeper and more perilous divide, expansiveness of the human spirit versus a violent contraction of it, an atavistic tribalism, often speaking, blasphemously, in the name of religion. More than ever artists and scientists know that they stand on the same side when it comes to the deepest meaning of culture.

I want to tell you a little bit about how it was that I first fell in love with science, with the idea of science. When I first learned how to read, I was given a library card and I made a strict rule for myself. Every trip to the library I would take out two books: one would be a make-believe storybook, because I loved make-believe stories. The other book would be a good-for-me book, not make-believe but something I could learn from. I was extremely strict with myself. I'd make myself finish the good-for-me book before I *allowed myself* to read the storybook. One-for-one, no cheating. I would get my books on Friday afternoon so that I would have them to read over shabbos.

One Friday afternoon I brought home from the library a good-for-me book called *Our Friend the Atom*, and this book really blew me away. It just shook the ramparts of my soul. Here's what I learned: The world was much farther away from me than I had known. I had thought that all I had to do was open my eyes and there it was, the pretty colored thing. But no, if I'd just opened my eyes I'd never have known about our friend the atom. I'd never have known that what the world really is is multitudes of neighborhoods of spinning atoms, of protons and neutrons and electrons and charges that came in three flavors, positive, negative and neutral. There was a whole lot more out there, a whole lot more *happening* out there, than I'd had any idea about.

But there was also less out there than I had thought. Those colors, for example, that I seemed to see out there, the blues and reds and my favorites, the yellows? Nope, not out there at all. The atoms were colorless. The book said so. It seemed to follow that those colors were only…where? They were in my mind, like dreams! What else was only in my mind then, and not out there, even though it might seem to be out there?

Suddenly it opened up in front of me: that vast abyss between how things seem and how they really are. How could you know how things really are? How did he know about this, the man who had written this great book, *Our Friend the Atom*?

The fact that science allows us to make this distinction between the way things seem and the way they really are, seemed to me, as a new reader with a library card, too wondrously amazing, and it still seems that way to me now. When I grew up a little bit I got to study relativity theory, that theory so beautiful that its theorizer knew even before he had the confirming evidence that it had to be true; and I learned that if you really take the physics seriously then the conclusion you must draw is that time doesn't really flow. Time is as still as spread space.

Time certainly *seems* to flow; it seems to fly: the present instantaneously here, and then slipping off into the irretrievable past. The flux seems the most distinctive fact there is about time, that fundamental difference between the uncertain future, the fleeting present, the unchangeable past. The temporal flux carries us all from vigorous youth to feeble old age, and that's only if we're lucky and get to be old. The flux is poignant, the flux is tragic, the flux is cruel, the flux is…unreal. The physics says so. Too wondrously amazing.

When Einstein was a frail old man he wrote a condolence note to the widow of a physicist who had been his friend, and tried to take the sting out of death by reiterating the consequences of his own physics: "To us believing physicists, the distinction between the past, the present and the future is an illusion, albeit a persistent one." Einstein took the logical consequences of his physics so seriously that it gave him the ultimate transcendence: freedom from fear of his own personal demise.

Escape from the confines of one's own puny little life, dedication to beauty, glimpses of transcendence. At the deepest layer, art and science are as merged with one another as are the beauty and truth that lies at their deepest structured level.

Is there anything at all in what I've said here today that is, well, Jewish? There are people in this room much better qualified than I to address this question and I'm afraid that they will. But I have to say that sometimes, almost against my wishes, even I suspect that there might be.

I've struggled most of my life to try to come up with a working definition of a good Jew, as I'm certain just about everyone else in this room has, too. By "working definition" I, of course, mean one that would work for me. A few years ago I came up with a notion of the good Jew that I like a lot: To be a good Jew means to be torn apart by conflict and contradictions, precisely because there is so much in this world to love—and some of these loves are very difficult, and some downright impossible, to reconcile with one another, meaning that we can't possibly give ourselves to them all. No, my friends, sadly we can't. But that doesn't make them any less lovable. And to deny their lovability is to falsify God's world.

Alicia Ostriker parenthetically mentioned last night (always pay attention to those parentheses) that she was surprised to learn that the hardest of the ten commandments is said to be the fifth, adjuring us to honor our parents. She said she'd always assumed that the hardest was the seventh, forbidding adultery.

Well, I'm solidly with Alicia on this one. In fact, I would argue that the better a Jew you are the harder it is to keep the seventh, because, being the good Jew that you are, you are vividly *attentive* to the sheer loveliness of so many. Of course, if you're a good Jew then you don't—you can't—give yourself to all the forms that loveliness takes; but because you're so very much aware of these myriad forms, because your soul quivers in exultant celebration of them all, well, the seventh is a doozy. We're meant to feel its dooziness—which is why I think that with all the many sub-groups we Jews have produced, all the liberties of interpretation that we've taken with the tradition, we've never gone in for asceticism, for that denial of our sensual nature, in love with sensual beauty, that would make keeping the seventh far too easy. *That* wouldn't be Jewish.

So to be a good Jew, I would argue, is to arduously attain that love of pure objectivity in which the accidents of precedents matter not a wit. That divine *apikorus* was a splendid Jew after all, as was Einstein. And to be a good Jew is to love one's own people, just as one loves one's own family—that is without much of any sort of good reason at all, certainly not for any reason that would lay claim on a purely objective human being. And loving one's people means loving their stories.

And so I love Jewish stories, as do all of you here. That doesn't preclude our loving all other stories as well. Of course we do, as good Jews. That is what is asked of us, what we ask of ourselves: out of ragingly conflicted souls, stretched wide by the force of loving in so many irreconcilable directions, that we be—that we write—Jewish.

REBECCA GOLDSTEIN *is the author of six books of fiction, including* The Mind-Body Problem, Mazel, *and* Properties of Light. *Her forthcoming* Incompleteness: The Paradox and Proof of Kurt Gödel *will be published in 2005. The recipient of many awards for writing and scholarship, including two National Jewish Books awards, she was named a MacArthur Fellow in 1996. She is Professor of Philosophy at Trinity College, Hartford* CT.

11. Fictions

Cynthia Ozick

Refugees

In 1935, when I was just eighteen, I entered the household of Rudolf Mitwisser, the scholar of Karaism. "The scholar of Karaism"—at that time I had no idea what that meant, or why it should be "the" instead of "a," or who Rudolf Mitwisser was. I understood only that he was the father of what seemed to be numerous children, and that he had come from Germany two years before. I knew these things from an advertisement in the Albany *Star*:

> Professor, arrived 1933 Berlin,
> children 3–14, requires assistant,
> relocate NYC. Respond Mitwisser,
> 22 Westerley.

It read like a telegram; Professor Mitwisser, I would soon learn, was parsimonious. The ad did not mention Elsa, his wife. Possibly he had forgotten about her.

In my letter of reply I said that I would be willing to go to New York, though it was not clear from the notice in the *Star* what sort of assistance was needed. Since the ad included the age of a very young child, was it a nanny that was desired? I said I would be pleased to take on the job of nanny.

It was Elsa, not Mitwisser, who initiated the interview—though, as it turned out, she was not in charge of it. In that family she was in charge of little enough. I rode the bus to a corner populated by a cluster of small shabby stores—grocery, shoemaker's, dry cleaner's, and 'under a tattered awning' a dim coffee shop vomiting out odors of some foul stuff frying. The windows of all these establishments were impenetrably dirty. Across the street a deserted gas station had long ago gone out of business: several large dogs scrabbled over the oil-blackened pavement and lifted their hind legs against the rusting pumps.

The address in the ad drew me along narrow old sidewalks fronting narrow old houses in what I had come to think of as the Albany style: part Hudson Gothic, part Dutch settler. But mainly old. There were bow-shaped stained-glass insets over all the doors. The lamps in the rooms behind them, glowing violet and amber through the lead-bordered segments of colored panes, shut me out. I thought of underground creatures kept from the light. It was November, getting on to an early dusk.

Frau Mitwisser led me into a tiny parlor so dark that it took some time before her face, small and timid as a vole's, glimmered into focus. "Forgive me," she began, "Rudi wishes not the waste of electricity. We have not so much money. We cannot pay much. Food and a bed and not so many dollars."

She was all apology: the slope of her shoulders, her fidgety hands twittering around her mouth, or reaching into the air for a phantom rope to haul her out of sight. Helplessly but somehow also slyly, she was reversing our mutual obligation—she appealing for my sympathy, I with the power to withhold it. It was hard to take in those pursed umlauts sprinkled through her vowels, and the throaty burr of her voice was lanced by pricks so sharp that I pulled back a little. She saw this and instantly begged my pardon.

"Forgive me," she said again. "It gives much difficulty with my accent. At my age to change the language is not so simple. You will see with my husband the very great difference. In his youth for four years he studies at Cambridge University in England, he becomes like an Englishman. You will see. But I…I do not have the—*wie nennt man das?*—the idiom."

Her last word was shattered by an enormous thud above our heads. I looked up: was the ceiling about to fall in on us? A second thud. A third.

"The big ones," Frau Mitwisser said. "They make a game, to jump from the top of the…*Kleiderschrank*, how you call this? I tell them every day 'no', but anyhow they jump."

This gave me a chance to restore us to business. "And the littler ones?" I asked. "Do you need help with them?"

In the dimness I glimpsed her bewilderment; it was as if she was begging for eclipse.

"No, no, we go to New York so Rudi is close to the big library. Here is for him so little. The committee, it is so very kind that they give us this house and also they make possible the work at the College, but now it is enough, Rudi must go to New York."

A gargantuan crash overhead: a drizzle of plaster dust landed on my sleeve.

"Forgive me," Frau Mitwisser said. "Better I go upstairs now, *nicht wahr*?"

She hurried out and left me alone in the dark. I buttoned up my coat; the interview, it seemed, was over. I had understood almost nothing. If they didn't want a nanny here, what did they want? On an angry impulse I switched on a lamp; the pale bulb cast a stingy yellow stain on a threadbare rug. From the condition of the sofa and an armchair, much abused, I gathered that "the big ones" were accustomed to assaulting the furniture downstairs as well as upstairs—or else what I was seeing was thrift-shop impoverishment. A woolen shawl covered a battered little side-table, and propped on it, in a flower-embossed heavy silver frame that contradicted all its surroundings, was a photograph—hand-tinted, gravely posed, redolent of some incomprehensible foreignness—of a dark-haired young woman in a high collar seated next to a very large plant. The plant's leaves were spear-shaped, serrated, and painted what must once have been a natural enough green, faded to the color of mud. The plant grew out of a great stone urn, on which the face and wings of a cherub were carved in relief.

I turned off the lamp and headed for the front door with its stained-glass inset, and was almost at the sidewalk (by now it was fully night) when I heard someone call, "Fräulein! Rose Meadows, you there! Come back!"

The dark figure of a giant stood in the unlit doorway. Those alien syllables—"Fräulein," yelled into the street like that—put me off. I disliked the foreignness of this house: Elsa Mitwisser's difficult and resentful English, the elitist solemnity of the silver frame and its photo, the makeshift hand-me-down sitting room. These were refugees; everything about them was bound to be makeshift, provisional, resentful.

Like a dog that has been whistled for, I followed him back into the house.

"Now we have light," he said in a voice so authoritatively god-like that it might just as well have boomed "Let there be light" at the beginning of the world. He fingered the lamp. Once again the faint yellow stain appeared on the rug and seeped through the room. "To dispel the blackness, yes? Our circumstances have also been black. They are not so easeful. You have already seen my nervous Elsa. So that is why she leaves it to me to finish the talk."

He was as far from resembling an Englishman as I could imagine. In spite of the readier flow of language (a hundred times readier than his wife's), he was German—densely, irrevocably German. My letter was in his hands: very large hands, with big flattened thumbs and coarse nails, strangely humped and striated—more a machinist's hands than a scholar's. In the niggardly light (twenty-five watts, I speculated) he seemed less gargantuan than the immense form in the doorway that had called me back from the street. But I was conscious of a force, of a man accustomed to dictating his conditions.

"My first requirement," Mitwisser said, "is your freedom to leave this place."

"I can do that," I said. "I'd like to."

"It is what *I* would like that is at issue. And what I would like is a certain engagement with—I will not say ideas. But you must be able to understand what I ask of you. What is this nonsense you write here about a nanny? How is this responsive?"

"Your ad mentioned children, so I thought—"

"You thought mistakenly. You should know that my work has to do precisely with opposition to the arrogance of received interpretation. Received interpretation is often enough simply error. Why should I not speak of my children? There is no context or relation in which they do not have a part. That is why your obligations will on occasion include them—but your primary duty is to me. And you will try not to disturb my poor wife."

It seemed, then, that I was hired—though I still did not know for what.

And it was not until a long time afterward that I learned that there had been (even in that period of crisis unemployment) no other applicants.

Even after two entire weeks, my position in the Mitwisser household remained amorphous, and if I attempted to ask what was expected of me, the answer was dissolved in chaos. "Just fill those boxes with papa's books," the oldest child ordered. Her name was Anneliese; she spoke good English—she spoke it casually, familiarly—though with a distinct accent. Except for the youngest, all the children had been enrolled, for some months now, in the Albany public schools. They had already acquired a patina of the local vernacular. It was several days before I could arrive at exactly how many Mitwisser children there were. They rushed around on this or that mission (the whole house was preparing for the move to New York); it was like trying to identify the number of fish swimming in a pond. At first I counted six, then four—the actual total was five. Their names were so many bird-chirps whirling around me: Anneliese, Heinrich, Gerhardt, Wilhelm, Waltraut. Waltraut was the easiest to remember, a round-eyed, curly-haired girl of three, who would cling to whoever happened to be passing by. Mrs. Mitwisser (I had given up trying to call her Frau Mitwisser) was not often seen. She was hidden in a bedroom upstairs and appeared to have little to do with the fierce activity all around.

I could not distinguish Heinrich from Wilhelm, or Gerhardt

from Heinrich. This was made all the more difficult because now and then they addressed one another as Hank, Bill, and Jerry, and then would rapidly switch back to Heinz, Willi, and Gert. "Papa doesn't like it when they do that," Anneliese instructed me. "Papa is a purist." Anneliese was sixteen, and regal. It came to me that it could not have been Anneliese who had jumped from the *Kleiderschrank* and loosed the ceiling plaster down below. She was tall, an inheritance from her father, and like him she gave out a formal strictness. She was hardly like a child at all; her hair was wound in braids on either side of her head, revealing tidy pink ears. In each lobe a bright dot glittered. Braided and earringed, she looked formidable and amazingly foreign; the three boys seemed more afraid of her than of their mother. They obeyed Mitwisser, and they obeyed Anneliese. But when Mrs. Mitwisser appealed to them—usually it was to beg them to take charge of Waltraut—they laughed and ran away. "American savages!" Mitwisser roared at them. "*Rote Indianer!*"

I too was careful to obey Anneliese. I felt my fate was in her hands: she alone, so far, had troubled to acknowledge my status as more than an intruder. The boys never spoke to me, nor I to them. They flew past me, heaving bundles into the vestibule, where a growing mound of objects awaited the movers. But my dependence on Anneliese went beyond her occasional command. She was the sole source of my understanding, incomplete as it was, of the annals of her family. I was startled to discover that timid Mrs. Mitwisser, whose eyelids were so red, and whose thin nostrils trembled like a rabbit's, had held a senior fellowship at the Kaiser Wilhelm Institute in Berlin.

"They threw her out," Anneliese explained, "and they threw papa out of the University. The Quakers brought us over, that's why we're here. Mama says they saved us. Papa says sometimes mama acts as if she doesn't like being saved, she won't learn English. But anyhow there was a mistake."

The mistake was comical. In their good-hearted intent to rescue a family of refugees, the Board of the Hudson Valley Friends College had requested its provost to invite Professor Rudolf Mitwisser, the well-known German specialist in the history of religion, to teach several seminars on the Charismites, a sixteenth-century mystical Christian sect, an offshoot of the Pneuma Brothers of northeastern Bavaria. The Board, businessmen mainly, had confused the Charismites—famous for their emphasis on the Spirit Within, akin to the Friends' Inner Light—with the Karaites.

I asked Anneliese who the Karaites were.

"Oh, they're just papa's people, some old Jewish heretics, they've been dead a thousand years. Papa likes them because no one else does. But it didn't matter about the mistake, the Board got us out and gave papa the job. He didn't mind about the Charismites. And they rented this house for us. Here, look, I sent Gerhardt for the rope you're going to need."

She handed me a scissors and a rough hairy coil. I had been packing books all that day, as she had directed me to do. There were thirty-two boxes filled with Mitwisser's strange indecipherable volumes, and in order to cram as many books as possible into each container I had arranged them in rows and towers, meticulously, according to their sizes and shapes. The rope scored and burned my palms as I tied the boxes shut.

Half an hour later Anneliese informed me that her father was not pleased, and after a moment he arrived to tell me so himself. His hands, with their great workman's thumbs, were soot-blackened. He had been sorting papers stored in the coal bin, he said; his eyebrows stood up furiously, like a forest of sooty straws.

"Why am I interrupted by such nonsense? Anneliese! This is how an intelligent creature organizes scholarship? By how tall and how short?"

I protested, "I had to make the books fit in the boxes."

"They must fit by idea, by logic. Ach, what cataclysm, what foolishness. You disrupt an entire library, Fräulein! And you, Anneliese, you permitted this?"

I was helpless: the books were in German, and in languages I could not recognize. I saw then that it would not always be safe to take orders from Anneliese; she was not above falling into error and disgrace.

"Anneliese," Mitwisser growled, "you must undo the boxes and begin again. Give to Fräulein Meadows a simpler task, one that she will not make into a wilderness."

The New York we came to was hardly the New York I had imagined. I was disappointed and astonished. I knew the city only from picture postcards and the movies, and in the movies (no one ever said "film" in those years) the opening scenes of airy skyscrapers and streaming crowds were always accompanied by syncopations of ascending horns and jazzy excitements. To me, and to all the world, New York was the peopled channels of Manhattan, and tall skies where no birds flew. And hadn't Mrs. Mitwisser, in that distracted attempt at an interview, hinted that the very point of the move to New York was her husband's wish to be near "the big library"? The big library of New York was on Fifth Avenue in Manhattan, fronted by two stone lions, like some Venetian palace. I had seen photographs of it. The place we settled in had no big library. It had no library at all; it had nothing. Compared to Albany, it was an obscure little village in a remote corner of the sparse and weedy northeast Bronx. Strictly speaking, the Bronx *was* New York, or at least an official part of it; but I felt deceived. The subway line had only recently crawled to this huddle of small houses hemmed in by swamp and creek—and yet there was, despite the name, no subway either: rather, a raucous elevated track that further darkened the fly-specked stores below, and finally nosed its way underground toward Manhattan only after what seemed scores of miles. The true New York was far away. Infrequent trains—toys high up on a trestle—were our only conduit to the promised city. Where were we really? A modest bay flowing in from Long Island Sound, with a ragged fringe of mud and sand and seaweed-mantled rock, defined a neighborhood ringed by open fields: beyond the city's caring, and out of its sight. Here were uncombed meadows purpled and gilded by violets and dandelions, and the drooping heads, with their insect like antlers, of wild tiger lilies.

Our house—rented and furnished—was one of an identical row: stucco flanks, a stoop, a green front door leading into a sun parlor no bigger than a cube (where no sun could penetrate). Within our first hour the largest room, on the second floor and at the back, was designated as Mitwisser's study; a wide bed stood against one wall.

The three boys were distributed between two rooms; Gerhardt and Wilhelm took one, and Heinrich, the oldest, was put in with Waltraut. Anneliese had her own room, across a narrow hall from her father. And in a cranny at the top of the house—she was deemed unfit for her husband's bed—I was made to join Mrs. Mitwisser. She had sunk into an ongoing strangeness, something deeper than lethargy, and more perplexing. She was unwilling to be touched by anyone—she pushed Waltraut away from her like a contaminant. Waltraut had grown used to these rebuffs, and would shrink at the first sound of her mother's footsteps. At night, alone with Mrs. Mitwisser, I would listen to her whimper; she murmured and hissed in her own language, the choked gurgle of a dammed-up river.

"Did mama sleep at all last night?" Anneliese asked. "Papa wants to know."

Mitwisser himself never approached me with this question or any other. It seemed I did not much occupy his mind; but more and more he occupied mine.

Meanwhile his wife lay on her bed in her nightgown. Sometimes she pulled out a pack of cards from under her pillow and idly shuffled them; or else she would lay them out in curiously unequal rows.

One afternoon I heard her singing:

Röslein, Röslein, Röslein rot,
Röslein auf der Heide—

She broke off and called me to her side.

"Röslein," she said, "that is your name, no?"

I said it was something like that, though in fact I could hear no resemblance.

"My husband told to me we have in this place a garden."

"There's a little back yard."

"Then we go there."

But she would not get out of her nightgown or put on her shoes, and Anneliese would not allow her to walk out as she was; so she went back to her bed, sullen.

"Mama's very bad this time, but at home it was worse. When they threw her out of the Institute she was *very* bad."

It was even more serious, Anneliese said, when they had to leave Berlin, they had to run away practically, it was a miracle they could ship out her father's books, first to Stockholm where they stayed for a month with a great-uncle, and then, when the Quakers intervened to save them, to Albany. In Albany their mother was almost all better, and Waltraut was happy, and the boys behaved themselves, and got funny new American names, and everything was nice for a while; but when the move to New York was decided on, little by little she worsened. And now she was very bad. That was how it was with their mother, she had a sickness, a private sickness—"Papa doesn't let us talk about it to anyone, only to our own family, and the nurse we had at home after they threw her out of the Institute, and then the law came that no German could live with us, so the nurse had to go away. And so did Waltraut's nanny, even though she was French."

"But you *haven't* moved to New York," I pointed out.

They almost had. But at the last minute their father had determined it would not be feasible, not with their mother so sick: what she needed was healing air, strolls, greenery. Sunlight and breezes. A quiet neighborhood, a backwater, a touch of salubrious scenery, no city swarms or city noises: it would be a kind of spa, and so much cheaper than Manhattan: as for Mitwisser himself, he would ride the subway to the Venetian palace that was the great library of New York.

All this reminded me of money. I had not yet been paid my salary; I did not know what my salary would be. "I guess you can barely afford *me*," I said.

Anneliese seemed offended; she turned aloof. Her cold eye told me I had transgressed. A redness flooded her forehead and ears. "At home we had things. At home we were all right. Here we have nothing. Papa's books we got out to Stockholm just in time, because of Uncle Sigmund. So now we have nothing if nobody helps."

"The Quakers—"

"Papa left his position. It's finished."

And so was our discussion; Anneliese's mouth tightened into

a flat line, like an oscilloscope shut down. "Go see about mama, please."

I saw then that the Mitwisser family was an impregnable fiefdom, with guards at the borders. No one could be admitted. No routine could be violated. Anneliese managed the household. Mitwisser went away every morning; though it was late June, he wore his heavy black suit and his red-and-black striped tie and his black fedora. He climbed the high stairs to the tracks; the train's screech bore him away to the unimaginable city.

And from her bed Mrs. Mitwisser resumed her mournful singing: "*Röslein, Röslein, Röslein rot...*"

I said, "Is it a lullaby?"

She did not reply; the singing went on. "*Röslein auf der Heide...*"

"Do you ever sing it to Waltraut?"

She was all at once fiercely, contemptuously alert. "The Fräulein does not know when she hears him it is Goethe! *Natürlich*, the child must not make a noise. When we go with the chauffeur in the auto. We go in the streets around and around. Gert and Heinz and Willi, my husband gives to them *Spielkarten*—" She released a sly brown look and reached under her pillow. Out came the pack of cards. "Will you like a little to play?"

That night I asked Anneliese about the chauffeured car.

"Papa hired it. It had smoked glass windows, no one could see inside." She turned from me and looked all around; but we were alone. "Only important people would ride in an auto like that, big and black, and the driver had a black cap with a shiny beak, like a policeman." And so for a week they were—precariously—safe. All over Berlin, Anneliese said, there were impromptu raids; people were being arrested right out of their own apartments, or the apartments of relatives or friends, wherever they tried to hide. You could be picked up at any hour, you never knew when or where, and there were still seven days before the ship to Sweden, they had their papers all ready, but where could they go in the meantime? Not home, not anywhere. "Papa gave this man, his name was Fritz, papa gave him the key to our apartment and told him he could take away anything he wanted, anything at all, if he would drive us around the city for a few days. Waltraut was so little then, she cried all the time, and mama had to sing to her, and the boys played cards, and we went up and down the streets day after day, and no one stopped us because the auto looked so important and official and dark. Fritz brought us food to eat in the auto, and when we needed to use the toilet we would hold our heads up and walk into any fine hotel. It made us nervous to do that, even though we were wearing our best clothes on purpose, and Fritz would get angry when Waltraut's diapers smelled bad, so we were afraid of him."

Anneliese spread her clean fingers into the shape of a fan and stared into the empty spaces between them. "He didn't trust papa about the key. Once he parked right in front of our own building and locked us all in the auto and went into the elevator and upstairs to make sure that it was really the key to our apartment. And when he came back down he told us that just next door he'd heard terrible screams, and when he looked in he saw some men beating an old woman and dragging her across the floor. Mama said 'Frau Blumenthal!' and papa said to keep quiet, and then Fritz said, 'Your place has paintings on the walls, what right do you people have to live like that?'"

She doubled up the fingers of her hand into a fist.

"So we kept on driving round and round Berlin, until the last day before the ship to Sweden was due in Hamburg—it took six hours, that part, getting to Hamburg, and halfway there, when it was still country villages and little towns, Fritz stopped the auto and said he wouldn't take us any farther unless mama gave him her wedding ring, and he made the boys and me turn out our pockets to see if we were hiding anything, and he tore off Waltraut's diaper. Mama was carrying her mother's picture in her bag, an old photo in a silver frame, and Fritz grabbed it, but mama lied and said the frame was only plate, so he threw it down. At the pier in Hamburg he asked papa for some more marks, and then he told us to get out finally, and that was that. Whether there was anything left in our apartment when he got back there with papa's key we never knew.—Waltraut will want some water, won't she, before she falls asleep, so take care of it now, please."

And after that Anneliese never again disclosed any part of her family's travail.

Summer had brought a heat wave that lasted for days. In the mornings Mitwisser would depart wearing his thick felt hat as usual, but with his jacket over his arm: the relentless early sun, already merciless, had the power to unbutton his formality. The nights were worse; the roof tiles had been absorbing torrid scorchings for hours, and there was not an electric fan in the house.

Little by little Mitwisser's cause was revealed to me. It was almost as if he was the muse of that stifling airlessness, those oven-like seizures: boiling rebellion was his subject. He was drawn to schismatics, fiery apostates—the lunatics of history. Below the scholar's skin a wild bellows panted, filling and emptying its burning pouch; a flaming furnace exhaled fevers. It was not August's torch that spilled the sweat from our necks. It was Mitwisser's own conflagration, invading, heaping up a pyre of libraries beyond his narrowed horizon: Cairo, Leningrad, London, the irretrievable Berlin. New York disgorged for him what it could. But—by now—what did it matter? He had become his own archive. Babylonia, Persia, Byzantium teemed in the sockets of his eyes; choirs of esoteric names rang out. I grew used to hearing the twisted Egyptian music of al-Barqamani, al-Kirkisani, ibn Saghir, al Maghribi. His Karaites! He was besotted, he was a repository of centuries, a courier of alphabets and histories.

One night visitors came. They came at ten o'clock, when Waltraut and the boys were asleep. I had already buttoned Mrs. Mitwisser into her nightgown; my duty was below. Anneliese had instructed me to stand at the green front door and guide the visitors into the dining room. Earlier I had set out teacups all around the scarred oak table, where the family, except for Mrs. Mitwisser, habitually had dinner. "Not like that," Anneliese scolded. She removed the tea things and laid out a white tablecloth. The occasion was to be an elevated one. Six or eight men filed in; one wore a yarmulke. They had arrived nearly simultaneously, in two cars, and appeared to be all of an age—between forty-five and sixty. It was the first time since I had entered the Mitwissers' insular fortress that strangers were being entertained. And still there was no air of welcome, or even of invitation; it was more a convention than a visit. The men exchanged familiar grunts and settled into their chairs while Anneliese and I handed out plates of miniature frosted cakes. I marveled at these cakes: they were not our ordinary fare. But the cups were chipped, and mazy brown cracks meandered over them.

I poured the water directly from the kitchen kettle. Anneliese whispered, "The teapot! Use the teapot, can't you?"—with such ferocity that I began to understand that some ceremony was under way. Was it to be a down-at-the-heels echo of those Berlin salons where Mitwisser had been feted? Was it a celebration, a commendation? The tea darkened in the pot. The little cakes with their sugar-whorl crowns gleamed. The visitors murmured, indifferent, detached, waiting.

"Go up and let papa know they're here," Anneliese said finally.

Mitwisser was standing in the middle of his study with a brush; he was brushing the jacket of his suit.

"How many have come?" he asked.

"I think eight."

"Eight? Then four have declined."

So he had summoned them. This night was his own creation.

"Tell them I am just finishing a bit of writing. Tell them in ten minutes I join them."

He went on brushing. Whoever they were, he would be their master.

Anneliese had posted me just outside the dining room, with the teapot at the ready. I refilled the cups, and still Mitwisser did not come down. I had misjudged—there were seven visitors, not eight: a dozen had been summoned, and it was five who had declined. I took in that irregular row of drumming fingers and tightened shoulders fixed in a forward curve, and temples either bald or graying, lined with ridges. Even the youngest of them had darkly graven markings under the eyes. These were worn and creviced faces, accustomed to tedium, like a crew of salesmen biding their time before making their pitch. I was struck by the mildness of their patience. Only the man in the yarmulke showed a vague irritability, rolling and unrolling the tip of his mahogany beard with a stiffened thumb. The beard, together with the yarmulke, signaled an aspect of some practice or piety, and this set me to reflecting on how Mitwisser, a student of the history of religion, after all, was in his own life bare of any sign or vestige of belief. Yet his brain rocked with the metaphysics of long-ago believers, men for whom God was an unalterable Creator and Ruler—and still God was nowhere in that house. Like the biologist who is obsessed by the study of the very disease to which he is immune, Mitwisser had raised a wall between belief and the examination of belief.

That was what it all came to, then: this wall, which the others doubted, or condemned, or assailed.

When at last he stepped into the light, they stood up with a formal cordiality, and he shook hands with each man, one by one. He was wearing his freshly brushed suit-coat, though the molten heat was so intimately invasive that it crept into the ears and along the necks of the company: they had all torn open their collars, where the sweat pooled in the hollows of their clavicles. From the constraint of these unraveled visitors it seemed improbable, at first, that Mitwisser had met any of them in some former circumstance; or yet again perhaps he had, distantly, at one of those international congresses frequented by seminarians, or even on his home ground, at sessions of the *Religionswissenschaftliche Vereinigung*, in Berlin or Frankfurt or Heidelberg (or Prague, or Vienna) before world-upheaval had thrust him into this unlikely place. Or he may have confronted them only through some cautious yet abrasive correspondence. It was anyhow clear that he was familiar with their views and positions, whatever they were, as they were familiar with his. A dangerous awareness glowed between Mitwisser and the visitors: it was his imperial force that had compelled them to await him in the steaming heaviness of this equatorial room, where damp elbow pressed against damp elbow and the tea misted their eyeglasses with its own hot breath, and a secret savagery, like an ember rekindling, longed to break out. The man in the yarmulke, it developed, was Viennese. A white-nosed fellow with a deformed left hand was revealed to be a specialist in tenth-century Egypt; with his good hand he quietly plucked a cigar out of his moist shirt pocket and sucked at it with so much diligence that he soon had the ceiling befogged. This encouraged the cigarette smokers, and since there were no ashtrays to be had (these were as foreign to the house as electric fans), I ran around the table dealing out extra saucers to catch the burnt-out stubs.

The bearded Viennese had started off, diffidently enough, in German. In all that smoke and swelter I saw how this aroused them, though I could detect no plausible link between the ordinary plainness of these men (except for the yarmulke and the bad hand, it was pointless to try to distinguish one from the other) and the turbulence that was beginning to spiral out of their suddenly violent mouths. These mouths, which had seemed so flat and contained, like the mouths of shrewdly affable grocers, were now wildly twisting and spewing, a gathering tornado of virulence. Or they were like the mouths of sideshow magicians who draw out strings of colored cloth flags from their throats, endlessly, an infinitude of flags. But these were not innocent flags; they were brutally pelting philosophies.

Intellect engenders meaning: interpretation; commentary; parable; illumination; insight; dialogue; argument; corroboration; demurral; debate; irony; anecdote; analysis; analogy; classification; clarification. All these the Karaites repudiate as embroidery and fraudulence in the hands of their enemies (though not in their own hands). And all these are Talmud, the first layer of which is Mishnah, containing commentary on Scripture, and the second layer of which is Gemara, containing commentary on Mishnah. The exegetical voices calling to one another across the centuries grow more and more populous, denser and denser. A third-century sage will contradict a first-century sage; a fourth-century sage will disagree, and take the side of the first-century sage. A fifth-century sage will hold to a new idea altogether. If you were to stand on a mountain—Mount Tabor, say, or even Olympus—and turn your ear downward toward where the minds of the philosophers reside, you would hear the roar of impassioned colloquy below, like a wakening polyphonic thunder. And this would be Talmud, the fugue-like music of the rabbis conferring over the sense of a syllable out of Genesis.

All this the Karaites refuse and deny. In the ninth century they become the rabbis' foes. Scripture! they cry, Scripture alone! They will not tolerate rabbinic interpretation. They will not allow rabbinic commentary. They scorn metaphor and the poetry of inference. Only the utterance of Scripture itself is the heritage divine!

The rabbis (whom the Karaites call the Rabbanites, or the school of thought that clings to the rabbis) reject the Karaites as literalists. The Karaites, they say, see only the letters; they do not see the halo of meaning that glows around the letters.

The Karaites ridicule the Rabbanites. They ridicule them because the Rabbanites declare that the Talmud, which they name the Oral Torah, was received on Sinai by Moses together with Scripture, the Written Torah. The Rabbanites claim that the sacredness of the Oral Torah is equal to the sacredness of the Written Torah.

Literalists! retort the Rabbanites. Narrow hearts! At Sinai the minds of men were given the power to read the mind of God. Otherwise how would men know how to be civilized? How would we know how to understand a sentence—or a story—in Scripture?

You understand it twenty different ways! scoff the Karaites. One says one thing, another says another thing. And this clamor of contradiction you call equal to the Torah itself!

It is equal, the Rabbanites respond, because the radiance of Torah directs men's thoughts. Out of the soil of strenuous cogitation, which is the engine of holy inspiration, and which you Karaites demean as mere contradiction, burst the sweet buds of Conduct and Conscience. The Rational Mind is the Inspired Mind.

The Rational Mind, argue the Karaites (but they do not notice that they are arguing Talmudically, since Talmudic argument is what they disdain)—the Rational Mind will not accept that the so-called Oral Torah, codified by human hands recording human opinions, is equal to the Written Torah given by God to Moses at Sinai! You Rabbanites indulge yourselves in delusion. There is in you no law of logic. Hence we depart from you, we reject all ordinances and adornments, inferences and digressions, alleviations and mildnesses, that are not in the Written Torah. We sweep away your late-grown lyrics that have crept into your prayer books. Our liturgy draws purely from Scripture, not a jot or tittle of it man-made! Away with your late-grown poets, away with your late-grown jurists! Moses alone stood on Sinai!

Thus spake the Karaites. But the Jews until this day embrace the Rabbanites and their ocean of exegesis and disputation, of lore and parable, as fertile and limitless as the cosmos itself—while the Karaites are a speck, a dot, a desiccated rumor, on the underside of history. Sa'adia Gaon, in the tenth century, in his famous polemic against the Karaites, blew them with a puff of his lips into the darkness of schism.

They were fighting him. They had come to fight him. They had come because he had summoned them to fight, and they felt the old vestigial power of his call; or because they were led by the dark curiosity that trawls minds to the grotesque, or the superseded, or the discarded, or the openly perverse; or because of their own volcanic anger. They raged against his will, his obsession, his desire—his thought. He was a violator (but he believed himself violated by world-upheaval, by their accusations, by their doubting enmity); his purpose, they said, was to subvert, to overthrow. He had deserted the green and fertile furrow, he had turned passionate, he had left disinterestedness behind, he had ruptured the Olympian surface of the scholar's detachment, he had submerged the distinction between the investigator and the investigated, the hunter and the hunted; he had become the quarry, he had flung himself into the hearts of his prey. He had broken through the wall he had professed—the wall between belief and the examination of belief. A false profession. He had the smell of a renegade.

The white-nosed man with the bad hand dropped his cigar. A cry—high-pitched and sharp, a treble upstairs shock—was shooting through the smoke.

"Waltraut," Anneliese whispered, "all this noise, it woke her—"

But I kept my place under the dining room lintel. "Leave her be, she'll fall back—"

"Go and see!" Anneliese commanded.

I kept my place. It was Mitwisser I wanted to see. He stood—he had never taken a chair—under the spell of a resignation concentrated and embattled but strangely tranquil: a ship captain who is unsurprised by a squall. He looked satisfied; I was certain he was satisfied. If you court the sea there will likely be a storm, and he had courted the sea, he had *made* the storm, he was the god of the storm, he was satisfied!

Again that cry: now it was descending the stair, now it had thinned to tiny breathless phantom moans enveloping a barefoot figure. Like a bird in a rush of wind, Mrs. Mitwisser flew into the room.

"Gentlemen, it's no good, no use"—she pulled and pulled at the torn breast of her nightgown—"no good at all—"

The visitors fell into a motionless silence.

"My dear Elsa," Mitwisser said.

"No good at all," she chanted, "no use, no good—"

"Mama," Anneliese pleaded.

"What is broken, gentlemen, you cannot put it again back, *nicht wahr?*"

The visitors rose in a body and mutely trickled out the door; only the man in the yarmulke hesitated before Mrs. Mitwisser. "*Guten Abend,*" he said.

"*Guten Abend,*" she replied: a chatelaine presiding over farewells after an evening of delicacies and wine.

Anneliese took her mother's hand and began to lead her away. Mitwisser's enameled blue eye trailed after them: his face blazed. "Quite right," he said. I hardly knew what he meant by this; I was thinking what an oddity it was that he had ever lain beside the woman in the torn nightgown. He turned back to me with a little shrug of surprise, as if he had just discovered me there. "You see how it is," he said. "I have no peers in this matter. What lies beyond the usual is dismissed, it is regarded as wasteful and perverse. They judge it—my work—to be pointless. What was once valued there is not valued here. Here they already lack the European mind, they are small."

"But isn't one of them from Vienna—"

"They are all, so to speak, from Vienna. And that one is no one at all. I will return now to my study. Please to shut off all these lights." He gestured toward the kitchen, where the kettle still steamed, and reached out himself to the dining room switch.

He left me in the dark, among empty cups and littered plates.

This was how, dimly, dimly, and little by little, I derived the nature of the Karaites at my typewriter at night, to the chanting of Mitwisser's esoteric recitations.

And dimly, dimly, and little by little, like ink bleeding through paper, I came to believe that of all the creatures on earth, it was only Mitwisser, Mitwisser alone, who thought to resurrect these ancient dots and faded specks. Their living remnants might languish still, across from the Baltic Sea, or close to the Black and Caspian Seas, sequestered in queer European pockets; but they were shriveled, hidden, lost. Mitwisser's illuminations scarcely followed them there. Isfahan, Baghdad, Byzantium had seized his brain and driven it back, back—thirteen, fourteen, fifteen centuries back, into the muffled quarrels of sect after sect, doctrine upon doctrine. The Karaite laws of consanguinity and incest were more urgent to Mitwisser's gaze than the streets he walked on. These fevered and forgotten heretics and schismatics—their creeds and codes and calendars, their migrations and mutations, the long generations of their thinkers—these were his own.

Only his children mattered as much.

And I thought: refugees. The calamitous and tangled lives of refugees. Subverted, overthrown.

CYNTHIA OZICK *is the author of many works of fiction, essays, and short stories. The Puttermesser Papers, a novel, was a 1997 National Book Award finalist, and her essay collection,* Quarrel & Quandary, *won the 2001 National Book Critics Circle Award for criticism. Her short fiction has received four O. Henry First Prizes, and her play,* The Shawl, *was staged by Sidney Lumet. "Refugees" contains excerpts from her most recent novel,* Heir to the Glimmering World, *published by Houghton Mifflin (September 2004).*

Leslie Epstein

Ethiopia: A Prologue

Three thousand years ago the Queen of Sheba, having heard of the wisdom of Solomon, traveled to Jerusalem in a caravan laden with spices and gold and gemstones, in order to test that king with hard questions. He answered them all and dazzled her as well with his wealth, his servants, and his demeanor before the Lord. One day the queen came across a room in the palace that was floored in glass; thinking that she was about to step into a pool of water, she raised her skirts. The commentators maintain that Solomon tricked Sheba and brought her to his couch, but it would be surprising if this queen, the setter of riddles, did not know the difference between the surface of a mirror and that of a lake. In any case, once back in her homeland, she gave birth to a son. This was Menelik 1, "son of the wise man," who, once he had grown, set out to visit the father he had never known. The moment the king saw him he recognized, as in a mirror again, not only himself but—such was the boy's lithe-someness and graciousness of form—his own father, David. As the young man prepared for his journey, Solomon caused the first born sons of the priests and the elders to travel with him; some say that he was also accompanied by the Ark of the Covenant, which he had stolen from the Temple upon his departure. Thus did the glory of Zion pass from Jerusalem to Axum, and from the children of Israel to what the Ethiopian people to this day consider the embodiment of the kingdom of God: their nation and themselves.

A thousand years later another foreigner arrived at the gates of Jerusalem. This was Titus Flavius, son of Vespasian, who had come to finish his father's task of putting down the revolt of the Jews against the rule of Rome. At his command were four legions, equipped with engines for throwing darts, stones and javelins, together with catapults, siege towers, and battering rams. Over time this force made its way through wall after wall of the outlaying quarters, though the desperate Jews made new walls of their corpses to fill the breech. At last the tower of Antonia fell and the battle for the Temple itself began. The defenders were weakened less by the Romans than by treachery, dissent, and a famine so great they were forced to gnaw the leather from their shields. Still the two armies fought not only by day but in a darkness so thick it was impossible to tell one's friend from the enemy at one's hand. Titus, seeing the futility of further attack, and recognizing that his rams, after six days of ceaseless assault against the Temple could make no impression upon the vastness of its stones, ordered its gates set on fire. The blaze soon spread to the cloisters of the inner court and all their furnishings. Yet the battle, raging more fiercely than the flames, might have gone on without end had not a legionnaire, seized by what the historian Josephus called "a certain divine fury," thrown a burning brand through an open window of the holy house. Thus on the 9th of the month of Av, the same fatal day on which the king of the Babylonians had previously destroyed it, did the chief wonder of the world, God's dwelling, burn to the ground.

The slaughter that followed was so terrible and the conflagration within the city so great, that, as Josephus tells us, the flames that consumed the houses were quenched by their inhabitants' blood. In that chronicler's reckoning, eleven hundred thousand perished in the course of the war and ninety-seven thousand were taken captive; but of these last the aged and the ill were slain, those under seventeen sold into slavery, and still others sent off to work the Egyptian mines. The unluckiest, perhaps, became gifts to the provinces, where they were destroyed by wild beasts in the spectacles. The tallest, however, and the handsomest of body, were reserved for the procession of victory, which was to take place when the conqueror returned to Rome.

Had there ever been a triumph like it in the history of the empire? In all of the city not a person remained at home lest he miss a moment of the pageant. Vespasian and Titus, father and son, each crowned with laurel, sat on ivory thrones. All the wonders, the varied riches of the vanquished land, uprooted trees and strange specimens of animals, paraded before them. At the center were the treasures of the razed Temple: the golden table of the showbread and the silver trumpets of the jubilee; the gem-studded crowns and rare purple hangings; the Ark, with the scrolls of the Law; and towering over the heads of those who bore it, the great lamp with its septuple branches that, as Josephus reminds us, "represent the dignity of the number seven among the Jews." Next in the procession, and most acclaimed by the multitude, were the pageant carts. Some of these were as high as three or four stories and each depicted a scene from the recent war: the scaling of walls and their demolishment by machines; the stoning of the populace; the countryside laid waste; the slaughter and the supplication of the enemy; and finally, a miracle of ingenuity and workmanship, the Temple in actual flames, together with the burning houses that fell upon those that dwelled within them. In that fashion those who had remained at home and only wished they had taken part in the battle were made to feel they had actually been present, just as men and women of the modern world are transported to distant conflicts by devices the ancients could never have imagined.

And the conquered Jews? They came last, after the wooden ships, the armies of centuries and centurions, and the waving images of the gods. Among the captives was Simion of Gioras, the leader of the revolt, with the rope that would slay him already around his neck. With every step he was so harassed and tormented that he must have blessed the God of his people when in a sudden hush his suffering was brought to an end. Only then, according to custom, were the crowds free to take up the feasting of that festival day; while the Jews were led off, many of them to complete the work of the famed Colosseum and to begin the construction of the great arch that would celebrate the victory of Titus as well as their own ever-to-be lamented defeat.

⅀

Nothing endures, said Heraclitus, but change; and by way of example he remarked that no person can step into the same river twice. Nonetheless, men continue to build their memorials not from sand but from stone; and it is true that on occasion some monument will seem to stand against the flood, like a boulder against the river's rush. Yet that same Arch of Titus, thrust upward like a great pair of shoulders from the throbbing currents of modern Rome, will in time turn to dust. Even the Jews who built it, whose stubbornness in persisting has made them both hated and holy, in the way that some aged rock will become sacred in an aboriginal's eyes—even they must perish, as the Chaldeans perished, and the Canaanites.

Still, what the Greek philosopher neglected to mention was that since time is infinite and the atoms of water finite, sooner or later the bather must find himself in the precise mixture of elements in which he had previously splashed. Josephus himself seemed to sense this, for when writing of that terrible 9th day of Av, he spoke of an Age of Revolution, as if history were a wheel, endlessly repeating itself, even as it pulverized those caught beneath it. And not just Josephus. Who among us has not felt that he was once before submerged in the same tide of experience that surrounds him now? When was it? In childhood? In an altogether different life? Or did that clank of metal nozzle on metal fender, the swift swoop and dip and swoop of the telegraph line outside the train's gray window, the bark-bark-bark of an unseen Alsatian, occur not just to you but to others of the race whose senses—the ears, the eyes—you have for an instant been allowed to share?

There are optical illusions, flaws in the glass, tricks or twists in time. At Auschwitz, a museum now, the visitor might see a photograph of a mother and her children walking along a roadway between bent concrete posts and electrified wire, only to raise his head and realize that, beyond the image, he stands on the same path, hard against the same pylons. He might see as well a large photograph that the

68

Sonderkommando managed to take of themselves while burning their fellow Jews: the upright, living men, the strewn corpses, the smoke from the burning pyre—all against a backdrop of the slender trunks and full foliage of a line of trees. Now raise the eyes: here is the same grove, limb for limb, branch for branch, notch for notch in the leafy crowns; only these trees are larger, thicker, taller, fully mature. Time not only captured, then, but as when only a few frames of a film are exposed each second, sped up, collapsed, turned instantaneously into history. Oh, poor witnesses! Poor trees!

In the summer of 1936, after two more turns of the millennial wheel, another triumph made its way along the avenues of Rome. The marching prisoners, barefoot and black-skinned, thought themselves children of the land of Israel. Among them, caged, was the last royal descendant of the union of Solomon and Sheba: the Emperor Haile Selassie I, *King of Kings, Lord of Lords, Conquering Lion of the tribe of Judah, Light of the World, Root of David, Elect of God*. For all the honorifics he stood with his uniform in tatters. At each lurch of his movable cage, his body swayed but, thought his hands were tied before him and a rope hung round his neck, never toppled. Indeed, his small, narrow head, with its tufted beard, its tangled hair, remained motionless atop the board of his shoulders.

What struck the milling masses—struck them so forcibly that they either fell silent or murmured, *occhi di Deo, occhi di marmo*—were his eyes, a strip of black iris, a strip of ivory white, and the way they stared as fixedly as those in a stone statue of Jupiter to where the great arch rose like a guillotine at the end of the Via Sacra. If those onyx eyes, wide and unblinking, possessed the power of the telescope lens they so much resembled, or could see on the wavelength of X-rays, the deposed king might have taken comfort from the image carved on one of the monument's inner walls; just as the new conqueror of Ethiopia, upright on the reviewing stand, his thumbs hooked in his leather belt and with no cap upon the bony pate of his shaven head, might have felt some unease at what had been carved on the other. For the artifacts of the vanquished people, carried along in a procession that mirrored the one now passing by, are all intact: the table of the showbread, the long-stemmed trumpets;

and, taller than the Roman soldiers who hold it aloft, the menorah, three new moons recumbent within three moons, symbolizing the city of Jerusalem, the light of learning, and the seven days of creation. Opposite, however, the goddess Nike reaches forward to crown the victorious Titus; alas, time has eaten away his head, so that the only laurel we see this day is the shadow of stubble that circles Mussolini's bullet-shaped skull.

LESLIE EPSTEIN *was born to a film family—his father and uncle wrote* Arsenic and Old Lace, The Man Who Came to Dinner, Yankee Doodle Dandy, Casablanca, *and dozens of other classic films. He has published nine books of fiction, including* King of the Jews, *which has become a classic of Holocaust literature, and the recent* San Remo Drive. *He lives in Brookline, Massachusetts, where for many years he has directed the Creative Writing Program at Boston University.*

Melvin Jules Bukiet

Return to Manhattan

The following scene takes place two thirds of the way into a novel-in-progress, but all you need to know is that Jefferson Weller is a non-Jewish American soldier who has just returned from his tour of duty in wwii and that Juliet is his sister. The narrator is Manhattan Island—mjb

Every town was crushed, obliterated. Ruins everywhere. But the people were happy to see us. Not only the French. The Germans, too. They'd been through Hell, at least I thought so, and it was over. At least I thought so. I remember one girl…" He fell into silent reverie.

"Yes?" Juliet prodded him ungently. She assumed that her brother was about to describe a romantic encounter with a pretty fraulein that made him understand the uselessness of war.

"She was a teenager and…"

Hell indeed, beyond Bosch. Bayonets carved open bellies and twisted round in intestines like forks in spaghetti. Rats crawled out of cadavers to wink at the living as if to say, "Your turn is next." In an attic in…oh, you know that one.

"I met her when…"

Rather than replicate the long pauses between clauses while Jefferson choked out his story, I'll tell it as I learned it the moment his ship made contact with dock #42. I knew it all the second he arrived.

71

The millisecond. The nanosecond. Email has nothing on me. Satellites, I don't need no stinkin' satellites.

Will the sky prove as stringent a boundary for me as the river? That's a different question. In the meantime, Juliet and I were both worried about why Jefferson had stopped writing, but neither of us could have imagined how worried we ought to have been.

He was physically healthy—we immediately conducted a visual survey to make sure that all his limbs were intact, the way a new mother automatically counts a new baby's fingers and toes. But a mother cannot peer into her child's soft cranium to make sure that he has all of his mental digits, and neither could Juliet. She had to wait for the words. I didn't.

Lieutenant (his letters didn't bother to mention a battlefield promotion) Jefferson Weller's mindscape was as blurry as rye whiskey and fifteen Seconal tablets—he popped a sixteenth—would make it a decade later. All he saw was smoke, because he kept looking at the sky rather than the awful images at ground level.

Indeed, one of his last thoughts prior to dropping off atop his heap of papers was of the pure spring afternoon in April 1945 when his column of troops marched less than a mile from the quaint, cobbled streets of Weimar to another universe.

Buchenwald they called it, world of beech trees. How lovely.

The entry house might have been a Swiss chalet—hot chocolate after a long day on the slopes. Constructed of the same timbered stucco as the cottages of the village that gave its name to the liberal republic that existed for a blink between the preliminary skirmish of World War I and the final solution of World War II, the villa was a sight to warm the heart. Unfortunately, its smell curdled the brain. Neither Lieutenant Weller nor any of the members of his platoon knew why their steps automatically slowed along the road to the *lager*, but their boots suddenly felt glued to the macadam. You can trust your feet.

Headless Private Carlyle had died next to then Private Weller in the Battle of the Bulge and hundreds of newly met friends and companions also died in close proximity to him as the Allied forces crossed northern Europe during the winter of '44–'45. In France,

Weller saw the devastation of combat, and in Germany he saw the wreckage created by air strikes in preparation for his arrival. Cologne was smoldering, and so was Dusseldorf, yet both of those cities were of a piece with the general havoc visited upon the continent. It all seemed the inevitable result of war. Buchenwald was different.

As Squadron 34c of the 4th Regiment of the 3rd Army under General Patton made its way eastward into the heart of the Fatherland, they began to hear rumors of a second war that they knew nothing about. The rumors were so extraordinary that they couldn't be believed, yet the eyes of the people who spread the rumors were dead serious, and the eyes of the teenage girl the Lieutenant found sitting in the roadway minutes before he entered the camp had no guile.

"Hello," he said to her.

"*Guten tag*," she replied, looking up from a game she was playing with several rough white cubes, oblivious to a thousand some men bearing down on her.

"Your name?" Lieutenant Weller asked in the primitive German he had learned over the last two hundred miles.

"Gretchen."

"What a pretty name."

"I am a pretty girl."

"And what are you doing here?"

She looked straight at him until he grew uneasy. Still, he must have passed some unspoken test because she answered "Betting game."

He didn't understand.

She explained, and he grasped enough to get the gist. The uneven cubes apparently chiseled out of some quartz-like stone were dice, but instead of bearing dots signifying numbers they were engraved with various emblems. One was a flower with a butterfly floating atop its petals, but the second was a gun, the third a knife, the fourth a rope, and the fifth a strand of barbed wire. The last and most mysterious side of the die was a cube within a cube. Lieutenant Weller rattled the dice in his fist.

"*Gehen wir auf geben?*" she said with a glimmer in her eyes as if the dusty roadway had been transformed into the green felt of a Vegas gambling table.

"Why not?"

She looked at him again as if he didn't understand. "Because games have consequences."

"And what is the consequence of this game?"

"That depends on what you roll."

He peered at the strange illustrations. "What happens if I roll the rope?" he asked.

"You're hung."

"And the gun?"

"You're shot," she replied straightforwardly. "By revolver in the neck or rifle at a distance, as you choose."

"It's good to know that I have a choice," he played along.

"Only on the gun. The others are what they are."

"The knife?" he asked, believing he already knew the answer he was bound to receive from this morbid child. How sad, he thought, that the war had warped the girl's imagination toward such violent fantasies.

She lifted up her skirt and revealed a knife strapped to her ankle.

"And what are you doing with that?"

"Just playing," she answered.

He looked at the die again, reluctant to ask what the other symbols meant, but he couldn't resist. "The wire?"

"Everything stays the same. Roll again."

"The flower?" he asked with trepidation, wondering if the butterfly was a bat.

The girl smiled. "That's the best of all. You go free."

You. He wondered whom she played this game with, but there was one more side of the cube: the enclosure or box. He pointed.

She yawned; that was the commonest of all. "Gas. You want to play?"

"No, thanks," the Lieutenant said. "Here." He opened his palm to return the gruesome game.

"Never mind, I have more," she said,

"Well, I have to go."

"Enjoy," she said, and the army moved on, into the forest that grew ranker and more acrid with every step.

※

Jefferson thought he had become inured to death, but Buchenwald taught him otherwise. The creatures who watched him enter the camp looked unlike any people he had ever seen. Their striped uniforms hung like rags on stick-figures. In places, their flesh adhered directly to their bones. Their eyes bulged out of their shaven heads.

All traditional markers of identity were missing from them. Some may once have been men and some women, but there was no telling the difference. Some, he discovered, were teenagers, but they all looked impossibly ancient. He couldn't distinguish any nationality in the murmuring babble of voices.

Several of Lieutenant Weller's troops vomited, but the prisoners in striped uniforms didn't seem to notice anything wrong, not the pall of smoke, not the bouquet of shit and decay, not the sight of bodies. Everywhere Weller looked there were bodies, or the shriveled remnants of bodies too fleshless to rot, individual bodies lost inside their baggy uniforms with only an outstretched hand and pencil-thin fingers to define their species, pairs of bodies that must have embraced seconds before their mutual demise, and stacks of bodies, heaped like cordwood in preparation for a harsh winter.

Several American journalists attached to the unit started snapping photographs to record what, in a moment of uncharacteristic modesty, they knew their words could never describe.

Years later, Weller still wondered if the photographers' desire to record these awful images were, as they claimed, faithful to a historical record or merely voyeuristic. But the people—Lieutenant Jefferson Weller had to keep reminding himself that beneath the rags and the scabs and the tattoos some of them bore on their left forearms these were people—whose pictures were being taken for the edification and disgust of the rest of humanity didn't seem to mind. As the one old man Lieutenant Weller eventually spoke to said with a shrug, "We've been through worse."

Their conversation started in June of 1945, several months after liberation. By then, Germany had officially surrendered and the Americans had become accustomed to their surroundings. The bodies awaiting the crematorium were buried in a mass grave lined with lime to keep infection from spreading. Every day, more of the former prisoners died of the effects of years of malnutrition or typhus which spread through the camp despite the efforts of teams of doctors, and they were accorded more individual burials. Everything about the strange new city of inmates and their liberators was gruesome, but it was more comfortable to live in a cemetery than an abattoir, and most of those who made it through the first few weeks returned to health.

Even the old man began to shed years as flesh returned to his face and hair to his head and a smile to his lips as several of the other creatures began to assume the appearance of living females. One in particular, Hettie Spokonie, a sharp-tongued orphan from Lithuania, made him blush.

Oddly, as color began to redden the survivors' cheeks, pallor took hold in the Americans assigned to nurse them. Lieutenant Weller lost his appetite when he heard stories from other survivors who drifted across Europe when Russian units threw open the gates to the scores of other camps in the concentrationary kingdom of the Reich. It swiftly became apparent that what they had in common, if not gender, nationality, or character traits, was religion; they were Jews.

Weller thought he was familiar with Jews, but the Hilly Island's immigrant or homegrown crop of the Chosen People was nothing like Europe's native produce. It didn't make a difference that Weller knew the sounds of Yiddish, as he did those of the dozen other languages in the Lower East Side's polyglot stew: Italian, Russian, Greek, etc., etc. Some of his own Irish-Americans even spoke archaic Gaelic to separate themselves from the Yankees whose vernacular reminded them of British lords. He knew the scent and taste of Jewish food—remember, the site of his last meal in the Western hemisphere was the Garden Cafeteria—and he had been a guest at dozens of Jewish weddings and bar mitzvahs and brises, the customs of which he knew as well as any rabbi, and he knew better than to schedule party meetings on the sacred fast of Yom Kippur, because the party faithful observed the holiday with a suckling pig feast in the basement of the Workman's Alliance Building on East Broadway. They violated every religious stricture they could, but they did so as mandated by the Jewish calendar.

Here, some of the Jews were Communist revolutionaries, but others were capitalist entrepreneurs, selling black market cigarettes within days of liberation. Some retained their ancient faith and some were agnostic or atheist. But all of them bore the ineradicable scar of their experiences during the last six years—even if the scar revealed itself in their refusal to acknowledge itself. Every hooked or Alpine sloped Jewish nose had inhaled the same stench of spilled blood and burnt flesh; every hooded or bright Jewish eye had seen that blood and that flesh. Every sharp and devious or calm and wise or dull and plodding Jewish brain—Jefferson did not believe in simple stereotypes—knew the same terrible truth. And that had changed them as it started to change him, too.

To begin with, he couldn't write anymore. He sat under the one tree in the camp his first night at Buchenwald and took out the notebook in which he had written hundreds of letters to Juliet. No matter where he had been on any given day of his war, at sea, on land, under bombardment or, during leave, sitting on a park bench with a fetching Welsh governess, shoulders close enough for static to jump from her cashmere cardigan to his uniform or thrilled by the volumes in the British Library, he had always found time to scribble a few lines to let his sister know that he was still alive and learning. The eternal student in him couldn't help but relish experience, good or bad, because it all went to make him a larger person. Yet he sat under the tree—an oak, I knew this from my own magnificent library, *The Life of Goethe* by Albert Bielschowsky, authorized translation from the German by William A. Cooper, G.P. Putnam's Sons, 1905—and was unable to use language to convey his thoughts to her or to himself.

He sat in the shade of the same tree under which the most emblematic Enlightenment intellectual had found inspiration. A green, spiral-bound notebook rested against his knees, a ballpoint pen held like a cigarette in his right hand, and all that came to his mind was...nothing.

Various figures walked along the paths of the camp: American and British soldiers on their way to the PX, Jews talking with great animation about the latest gossip about visas that filtered—the gossip and the visas—through a trans-continental grapevine, or romantically hand in hand, like teens at a summer camp, discovering the pleasures of the body. Sex was as rampant in the DP camps of Europe as it was the migrant labor camps of California.

Not that Lieutenant Weller shared the erotic impulse. Despite his English affair, he'd lost that ability, too, along with his appetite, along with any literary talent he once displayed in his letters. He was perennially exhausted, and had to drag himself out of his bunk to face the tasks of the morning.

The one action he was able to take was to sign a form that kept him in Europe instead of sending him home with the rest of the platoon. Shocking all the soldiers who had become his fellows on the march from Normandy to Buchenwald, he reenlisted.

"Writing?" the old man he had noticed on his arrival said one dusk at the base of Goethe's oak.

"Not really," Weller sighed.

"Why not?"

"I don't know what to write about."

"Not enough material?" the man smiled. His teeth were terrible and Weller considered recommending the division dentist.

"Too much."

The man nodded and walked away, but he returned a day later and the day after that until Weller began to expect his silent companionship.

Meanwhile, thousands of prisoners from other camps were swept into Buchenwald like so much lint into a dustpan before being dumped elsewhere, some to camps managed by representatives of Jewish self-help organizations, others into the Diaspora. Weller's days were busy with bureaucracy, which was a relief. As long as he was responsible for sending the correct requisition form to the quarter-master's corps for food and clothing for his charges, he didn't have to be responsible for their souls. He could leave that to a rabbinical regiment, some risen from the ranks of the survivors, some jetted in from American congregations, who thought that all the survivors needed to right themselves was a daily dose of Torah.

"I'm leaving," the old man said one evening.

Lieutenant Weller roused himself from their heretofore mutual silence. The man's hair had grown from his shaven head to cover the tops of his large ears and he wore a dapper fedora rescued from the camp's vast storage facilities called Canada because of its great natural resources. If the man was finally ready to talk, the least Jefferson could do was the same. "See you tomorrow."

"No, I don't mean for the night, until tomorrow. I'm leaving the *lager* and the camp and the country and the continent. Forever."

"Visa?"

"To America. It just came through."

"Congratulations."

"Are you going to stay here and not write?"

"It's worked so far."

"Or hasn't."

Weller nodded wry agreement.

"Advice?" the man asked.

"Why not?"

"Lie."

"Lie down?" Jefferson was confused. He could use the sleep. Nights, I later learned, tormented him. The bags under his eyes told Juliet as much as his words.

"You don't have to say any more," she urged him to be quiet.

"Oh, no, that's just the point. I do," he insisted, and continued with his story.

"Tell untruths," the Jew clarified.

The lieutenant furrowed his eyebrows. If he knew one thing about the Jewish people, it was that they were dedicated to the truth. That's what made them perfect revolutionary material.

"People are more likely to believe you," the Jew continued. "And the greater the lie, the greater the likelihood of belief. We, for example…" He gestured toward a crowd of survivors circled around a dark-skinned young man who had snuck into the camp to recruit them for illegal settlement in Palestine. "We told ourselves one lie about God four thousand years ago and this is where it got us." He gestured again to encompass the *lager*. "Now we're busy developing another lie to get ourselves through the next four thousand years."

Jefferson was shocked. He had been sympathetic to the organizers from the Middle East. They advocated a bootstraps socialist ethos similar to that of the Lower East Side, so the Lieutenant had looked the other way when they began proselytizing to the survivors.

Nearly a year after the war ended, the former prisoners were still effectively prisoners of the less lethal camps. Visas came through infrequently and only to those who had relatives in the United States willing to sign for them. Every time a handful slipped past the barbed wire, en route to the so-called Yishuv, the lieutenant mentally wished them well—and also had one less mouth to feed. "Wait," he said, "how did you get a visa?"

The Jew shrugged, "I lied."

❦

"If you really can't lie," the Jew continued, "the alternative is to find someone else's lie and write about that. Just make sure it's the biggest lie there is."

"I'll try," Jefferson said.

But the Jew was sure that the soldier would never have made it through a day at Buchenwald, and the next day, he was gone. He said he was leaving and he left. Another exit from Jefferson Weller's mind, another entrance to the Hilly Island. I noticed the latter the day it occurred, September 30, 1948, but I'd only connect it with the former after Jefferson returned, determined to follow the man's advice. For all the research that followed, for all the time spent at the Public Library and in the municipal archives scattered around a dozen basements off Foley Square, formerly Five Points, he never knew that the man who had set him in motion had set up a shop selling pipes three blocks away on Canal Street.

All Jefferson knew was that the Jew was gone. When another Jew entered his office later that day—what for, I don't know, Jefferson had no recollection—he couldn't help but bring up the subject. This was the last European conversation he was to have.

"I guess that visas will start to come through more often, now."

"We're still waiting."

"But at least one person got one."

"Cohen?"

"I don't know."

"He sat with you under the oak."

So the lieutenant and—what was that name, Cohen? Corn?—had been observed. Of course, these people missed nothing. It was a legacy from their days under the Germans when noticing a single chunk of rotting meat in their daily sludge meant the difference between nourishment and starvation. "Yes."

"You helped him?" The new Jew was there to find out how the old Jew had gotten out.

"No," the lieutenant said. "I mean, I would help anyone anyway that I could, but I couldn't. I assumed that he was...lucky."

"Lucky?" The man's eyebrows raised.

"Yes."

The American's puppy dog innocence was so obvious that the new Jew was convinced. Still, he had something more to say. "Luckier than you know."

"Well, any visa these days is..."

"That's not what I mean."

"What do you mean?"

"Cohen was the only one who ever won the game."

"The game?" All Jefferson could do was idiotically repeat the last lines of the Jew's sentences.

"A local pastime. One of the subkommandant's daughters invented a game to keep us amused. She had these dice made."

Weller felt a chill run down his back. He had seen the implements. "Special dice?"

"Very special. Instead of dots, one side had a gun, another a knife, another..."

"A rope."

"So you know how the game was played?"

He didn't know, and he didn't want to.

The Jew went on. "If you chose to play, you rolled the dice and your fate was…"

Weller couldn't stand the jaunty tone. He knew; he knew. "Sealed."

"Four out of the six were death. One was a tie. Stay where you are. And the last was freedom."

"Not very good odds."

"Better than others." The new Jew looked out the window of the office at the crowds milling about the bulletin board which listed inmates registered at other camps for a parent, a sibling, anyone from the same home town.

"How many people played?"

"You'd be surprised."

"I'm always surprised."

"Dozens, maybe more. It wasn't all that common because rumor had it that the odds were worse than one in six, that the die was loaded so that it never landed on freedom. But whenever anyone had had too much, he would send word through the guards that he was ready to play. The whole camp would gather for the event. A special table was set up, and we'd stand in rings to watch. Some people would trade cigarettes for a good position. But only when everyone else was ready would the girl make her appearance. She always wore a special white dress for the occasion, the executioner's gown."

Jefferson saw the smudge-faced teenage girl from the roadway in her gown.

"Six assistants preceded her in single file procession. One carried a revolver, one a noose, one a knife, and one a canister of Zyklon в."

Jefferson remembered the cube within the cube; it was a gas chamber.

"Those were the killers. One carried a strand of barbed wire to represent a tie; it meant stay where you are. And one carried a flower and a key."

"The key to the gate." Jefferson glanced toward the ornamental iron fence at the front of the camp.

"She carried the die like this." The Jew cupped his hands into a bowl. "The game was very ceremonial. She sat in one of the chairs and the player sat in the other. That, too, was special, because there were no other chairs in the camp. Still holding the die, she would explain the rules though everyone knew them, and then the player was allowed to lift the die from her hands. Sometimes, we placed bets on the result."

Jefferson saw the scene in his mind's eye.

"The player could take as long as he wanted and that too was remarkable. It was as if the sun stood still. But eventually, he'd have to toss the die. Sometimes the contestant threw it down, sometimes up, toward heaven. It might rattle as it rolled across the table, but when it stopped, fate was written. Five of the six assistants would retreat and one remain. If it was the gun, she would lift it—it was already loaded—and shoot right there. If it was the knife..."

"Stop."

"No, you must know everything."

"I know." Jefferson squirmed in his chair and closed his eyes though the scene unspooled behind his shut lids.

"Well, I suppose the knife and the noose are obvious. The gas was different than usual, however, because the chamber was prepared for one person alone. It usually held a few hundred. Then the girl would climb a ladder to the top and personally dump in the chemical. It was an honor, a solitary death, and I believe that many players secretly hoped for this result."

"And?" Jefferson couldn't help it. He wanted to know.

"Well, as I said, the barbed wire meant a tie. You were allowed to cancel the rest of the game or try again. But so many people were so excited that canceling was considered bad form. One gentleman, a banker from Antwerp, used to the bourse, threw four ties in a row, each time taking longer to roll the die. He caressed the cube for nearly an hour before his last throw. It was dusk. All activity had stopped in the camp and the rest of the guards came to watch. When he finally hit the knife, he sighed, and the girl pounced. What a tiger! They had to bring in a new table."

"And the flower, the butterflies." Weller needed to know that the evil game had at least once led to something good. Just once would be sufficient.

"Cohen," the Jew said. "He wasn't a Musselman. He hadn't given up on life. I think he was just curious, or maybe he figured out a secret way to throw the die, because when it left his hands, the thing didn't tumble or roll. It went to the table as if a magnet pulled it. Slap." He clapped his hands against his thighs.

Weller nearly jumped.

"No one could believe the result. The princess stared as if she saw her own doom there. She had never had to deliver anything but death and maybe she didn't know if she could, but the rules were the rules. She went to her father who went to the kommandant who laughed. 'Of course, you can let him go, but where will he go to?' Of course, he was right. The princess unlocked the gate, but Cohen refused to exit. And from then on, it was as if he was invisible. He ate, he slept, he froze in the winter when we marched on the parade ground, but the Germans never mentioned his number."

"That's because he told the biggest lie."

"What?"

"Nothing."

"Oh well, that's the story. Any questions?"

"One."

The Jew nodded and waited.

"What was the die made of?" Lieutenant Weller knew the answer to that one, too, before the Jew told him, but it was too big a lie to believe. It was time for the soldier to go home.

MELVIN JULES BUKIET's *ninth and most recent book is the collection* A Faker's Dozen. *He was the first Distinguished Visiting Writer at Bar Ilan University and regularly teaches at Sarah Lawrence College. He lives in Manhattan where nothing bad ever happens.*

III. Verse

Shirley Kaufman

Circle

For Aliza Auerbach

1 Passage

A sudden dazzle from above
as if a third eye, great disk of light
shines through the widened hole

and stuns the new child.
How does it get to the outside,
pushed from the sheltering cave,

muck and chaos of the dark canal,
ripped flesh left by its head
emerging? It enters history in blindness

not ready to see what the world is.
Memory begins its fine tracing in the brain
so even the frenzied thrust is recorded,

the panic already learned. Perhaps
the way out is always like this:
pressed through one's blindness

into the terrible dawn of light.

2 First Life

If you begin with terror, primal
cry of the new-born, eyes first blinking
from the womb-world into the unknown light,

if you begin with the cut that splits it
forever from its first home, blood slimy
on the face, the clutching fingers,

if you begin with a body's weight
first measured in the lifting arms,
a human touch to lessen the fright,

life becomes what it is and is not only
a slippery cord severed at both ends.

3 Last Life

The wrinkles on your mother's face track
her passage back to beginnings.
Creases run down the sides

of mountains when the ice thaws.
Nothing can stop them.
She is becoming a mountain.

Her separate selves are one now.
She bears them willingly like weather:
wind and salt spray, weathered love.

Her life is a circle in which she skates
down the hills with the children,
or swims in the sea every day

out and back to the crumbling shore.
The skin of the earth cracks
from the strain of holding itself together.

She keeps her wholeness.
Her wrinkles have a woman in them
brushing the light. It shines

where the luminous waves are braided
and fastened to the top of her head
with a comb. It shines on her hair.

SHIRLEY KAUFMAN *was born in Seattle, Washington and lived in San Francisco until 1973, when she immigrated to Jerusalem. Eight volumes of her poetry have been published in the USA, most recently* Roots in the Air: New and Selected Poems *(1996), and* Threshold *(2003). Her poems and translations have been widely anthologized. Her* Selected Poems, *translated into Hebrew by Aharon Shabtai, with Dan Pagis and Dan Miron, was published in 1995.*

Linda Zisquit

K'desha and Other Poems

K'desha (ke-day-sha): harlot, from *qadistu,* the pagan priestess of Baal and Astarte who engaged with holiness through her sexuality; related to the Hebrew *kadosh,* or holy (the same root as in *Kaddish,* the mourners' prayer).

K'DESHA

Once
in burning summer
on a night fierce with sirens
and still air
I let Rachmaninoff
pound the walls and open doors,
I sat on the step and could not
contain the sounds
to obey her, I couldn't stay
inside.
Through the dark
I drove along Buffalo streets
till the blinking strobe-
light of a man's apartment

beckoned, and not sure
of anything but her *don't*,
I parked and stepped off
the hardrock of one life
onto the slope of the next.

CONVALESCENT HOME

I

I couldn't sit still when I visited her,
rushing off as if I had an appointment—

now it seems every act was a show.
Even our walks by the canal behind the home

when I wheeled her around and pointed to birds
hovering over the water and named trees,

exotic flowers. I left her in the dining hall
during feedings: a lady among spoons clanging,

bibs on the overgrown kids
who swallowed their carrots and had their chins

wiped clean. I asked if she remembered
the day it happened, when her dying started.

Back in her room, the one with *Annie*
tacked on the door in childish script

I'd read to her, certain she wasn't listening.

2

Once I asked her if I looked the age of the author
and she said the name under the author's photo.

"Mom, you can read?" How little I expected
of her, as though nothing made a difference anymore—

Of course she could read, and looked up at me
quizzically as she used to.

from THE FACE IN THE WINDOW

❧

Was that you, Ma, really, at the end? I don't
mean the first time I accustomed my eyes
to the corridor lined with wheelchairs,
afghans and shrunken figures leaning to one side,
their white hair tight against the pinkish scalps
or sticking out in punk-like spikes, and spotting
you at the very end in your new smock
I started running to surprise you, imagining how
you'd smile, when from the side a tiny voice
called my name as I ran by. I turned and recognized
your patient face, your new voice that waited
till we were alone to accept my help, the first time
you said *yes*, when I asked should I come.
The face of the self-effacing is the hardest to see.
In the end those human sounds must be released,
need to be seen. I mean later, when it seemed
you were silent, beat, gone, and your ears kept on
as your body gave out, they refused to close down
till you'd let each one of us in, safe in sound.

❧

Maggid

I've invited them all in here:
the ones you suspected I slept with
and a few I kept out of view,
even the silent one and the rogue
who made it hard to leave Buffalo
then never showed up when you
died. You always thought I stole him
from a friend, you thought the worst
of me, I know, I gave you cause.
It's what we had between us.
But did I have to lie—
why couldn't we talk, or fight it out
in the open, or at least try
instead of burying us both alive—
now we're at this party together
you and me and the shades of all
my men, the muses of my sleep,
the fabric of my shroud, the prizes
I earned and hid, to keep your love.

AIRMAIL

A child
I fumbled in the dust
my fingers white and plump
inside the crumpled bag
till I reached rectangles
and square
after square
of thin airmail sheets
and on them your
familiar script,
the strips you licked
now ripped edges like the cliff
I once

jumped off in celebration
of separation.
I thought I'd suffocate
breathing them in again.
I opened one and then
another and around me
they fell like clouds
soft and gentle
as your voice had been.
Too late to return
to that city where I left you
writing letters,
how can I tell you
what I've learned?

LINDA ZISQUIT *was born in Buffalo,* NY, *educated at Tufts and Harvard, and has lived in Israel since 1978. Her third collection of poems* The Face in the Window *as well as an expanded volume of her translations from Yona Wallach's work were recently brought out by Sheep Meadow Press. She teaches in the MA in Creative Writing Program at Bar Ilan, and runs* Artspace, *a Jerusalem art gallery representing contemporary Israeli artists.*

Mark Rudman

Inside The Park: Lines on the Death of Billy Martin

Yankee Stadium

I
The Relay

Rounding third base, I see him
spiking the dirt, his powerful thick thighs
pumping; I had watched him round
second as the Kansas City center fielder
threw toward second base,
seeing, knowing, the utter hopelessness
of the effort; he was beaten before he rounded third, going
on pure bravado; *hauling ass*, not even for
glory—just to have his way; an *asshole*, I thought as…,
having torn his hat off, he rounded
third and the ball left the shortstop's hand—
the third base coach waving his arms
like a train signal for him to halt
take the easy triple—

I watched, and the dugout rose,
and he slid into home plate,
spikes flashing at the catcher's mask.
It was one of those doomed gestures.
A hush breathed through his futile strides.

The catcher and umpire, tense from waiting
for him to arrive, looked like turtles as they leaned forward,
while he looked skinned; *skinless.*

I caught the dejected look
on Martin's face as he trotted back out
to second base and the A's shortstop
tossed him his cap: a victim of cosmic injustice,
of a mistake in the order of things.

2

Seated in our box seats, above the dugout, we were
          orbiting the sun;
clouds were floating in azure over the dome of the stadium,
the mound, the outfield, the tawny infield dirt,
raked between innings.

We were the guests of the last place Kansas City A's
and they were losing badly.
I didn't care. I was now an Illinoian.
The White Sox, the giant killers, were my team:
bunt, steal, run, slide, sacrifice,
Luis Aparicio and Nelly Fox,
no grandstanding, no—power.
At least that scoreboard in Comiskey park in Chicago
responded with Oz-like fireworks and horns

when one of the Sox connected...

3

Everything in the game, except Martin's
gratuitous act, seemed predestined.
Martin only seemed small: he was taller than Mantle.
But Billy didn't wield his bat like a toothpick
and bang ball after ball into the high bleachers
during batting practice.
Billy didn't have power, only *cojones*.

Vic Power was the A's only All-Star.
Every time he came to the plate I was sure
he'd smash a ricocheting line-drive
off the left center field wall for a stand-up double—
and pause as he trotted back to second—
content with his effort—but also in despair at the waste
that his team would leave him stranded there.

(The great man theory of history ran aground here.)

Power was helpless to lift the A's out of the cellar.

Power was great but the Yankees were powerful.

They could afford to make mistakes.

4

I was there—I remember now at the hour of his death—
with some psychologists who worked for my father and my aunt,
and my father and my aunt,
who were also, that day, hosting their *team*
of "qualified specialists":
(the "Klein Institute" was administering psychological
aptitude tests to the A's).

The psychologists seemed utterly at ease
in the stadium, even if they were
dressed in dacron suits, didn't loosen their ties
and held briefcases to their chests. I felt
protected by their aplomb.
When A's slugger Gus Zernial smashed a thoughtless
     and peremptory
solo homer over the shortest right field fence in the majors,
I said: "He always does that, hits a homer
when it no longer matters for the team,"

and my father said, "You're right Mark, that's what the tests
show. I remember the name. Gus
Zernial."

5

"This is dullsville," my father said, erupting sometime late
in the 5th inning. "The game's over."
This was omnipotence and I,
a puny human, was overwhelmed
by the prophecy: to think that one can
know in advance, think of the grounder
as "routine"—they'd never been
routine for me throwing my whole body
like a glove over the ball at the hot corner,
but here, even though the ball moved
at this "dizzying" speed, a
phenomenal velocity, things
were stable, predictable—a smashing blow
into the blue—*routine*—not to be
lost in the sun, misjudged, hesitated
over.

Grownups knew things in advance.

But to what end other than to suck the suspense
out of anticipation?

6

It was Zernial's home run, making the score
Yankees 5, A's 1,
that wrecked the day.
Zernial's home run
seemed an unexceptional line drive down
the right field line that just cleared
the fence—while Martin's blow

to center field

was tremendous.

It wasn't Martin's fault that the center field wall
was farther from home plate than any other in a major league park,
461 feet…, and as the ball sailed off his bat
into the ether it hung suspended
as if the wind-gods were playing catch…;
he trotted to first thinking he'd hit a home run,
and tried to make up for it
on his way to second, tearing off his hat
when he heard the chant go up in the grandstand—

go, go, go.

And gone was the game's boredom and inertia.
in Martin's manic doomed and useless attempt.

Maggid

As Billy, out before he turned third, slid
into home, his empty, pointless, drastic gesture
brought home to me the slow ruin of everyone around me—

my red-haired aunt, her floral navy rayon dress
billowing in the awkward stop-time of the tag,
leaned forward to get my attention and say
"good game, eh?"
But it wasn't a question.

The psychologists, in a sweat, took off their jackets,
anxious now for the time to become unfrore again and for the game
        to end.
It was a day's work, being there.
(They had to be nudged when it was time to cheer.)

My father rolled up his sleeves and loosened his tie.
He placed his elbows on his knees.

It was bliss, earthly perfection, each time
they raked the infield dirt clean of cleat-marks.

7

If it hadn't been for Billy Martin I might not
have cast aside my catcher's mask
in Pony League practice in Salt Lake City
and taken Sarge's fastball in the forehead
when the ball eclipsed the flimsy insecure webbing of my cheap
Japanese catcher's mitt.

Something goes click in the brain:
you're expanding, exploding
the space of your body, touching

everything.

Whenever I witness or commit one of an uncountable number
of acts of hubris, or self-sabotage, I think:

It's like Billy Martin
who tried to beat a triple
into a home run.

MARK RUDMAN, *poet, essayist, and translator, has won a Guggenheim
fellowship, an* NEA *award, and the National Book Critics Circle Award.
He is the author of numerous books of poetry and prose including* The
Millennium Hotel, Provoked in Venice, Rider, Nowhere Steps, Realm
of Unknowing, Diverse Voices, *and, most recently,* The Couple.

IV. Fictions

Max Apple

House of the Lowered:
A Short Story

As soon as he heard that Carlos was coming to visit him before the 92nd shipped out to Iraq, Elario decided to throw a party. "Barbecue, mariachi, the works," he said, "the marine is landing in Houston." Though he rarely saw his son, Elario talked about him a lot. "Carlos always knew he had a father," he told me, "it wasn't much, sometimes maybe $10 a month, but every day of his life that boy knew he had a father who sent money."

I had to hand it to Elario, he'd come a long way. Two years ago when he asked for credit, I didn't even know his name, but I recognized him because he'd been coming in for a few weeks to window shop double quad speakers.

"Mr. Aaron," he said, "*el Diablo* needs sound, some blocks, and a skirt."

"You're talking close to a thousand," I said.

"I'm gonna give you this," he said, "for collateral."

He put into my hand a head shot of a teenage boy in a little frame that he pulled right off his keychain.

"Is this an antique or something?" I asked.

"That's Carlos," he said, "he's on the track team at San Antonio Union." I looked at it and I thought, this guy is not a good credit risk.

"Every weekend I'll work the money off," he said, "trees, lawns, plumbing, whatever you need."

I did have a lot of yard work so even though I knew better, I jacked up the price by twenty-five percent and gave him the credit. The next Saturday Elario showed up at my house in a 57 Chevy that I didn't think would ever make it out of the driveway. He'd lowered that Bel-Air coupe to maybe three inches over the road.

"You're risking your chrome on every pothole," I warned him.

"You're right," he said, "but what can I do? The snake loves it." He pointed to the reptile on his left arm. I saw that particular tattoo on lots of gang members, and in various colors. Elario had the long model, shoulder all the way to his wrist with the snake's head on the back of his hand. "Who's running the show?" I asked him, "you or the snake?" He laughed about that the whole time he worked on my flowerbeds.

In a hundred years I would never have thought that someone like Elario would end up in the store, but when I put out the help wanted sign he had already worked off his credit so I gave him a shot at the job. Maybe he has cost me a few sales because of those gold chains and his partly chewed off ear, but most of our customers come from the barrio and, like I told him, I believe that by all rights Houston should still be part of Mexico.

He disagreed. The Mexican cops were worse he said. Everyone was on the take and the judges were all whores. At least in Houston after a few days you could make a decent bail arrangement. But that was all in his past. I trust Elario every day with the cash register and a lot more.

When I needed help with mom, Elario was the one who came through. He brought over his own mother, Luisa, from somewhere near Oaxaca. He took five days off work; drove down there and then snuck her over the border. Don't ask—don't tell is my policy too.

"She's strong and clean," he said, "she can carry a sofa on her back, I've seen her do that, but back home she can't earn a dollar an hour." I had had it with one agency hire after another not showing up to take care of my mother who has Alzheimer's but is okay below the neck. She just can't be left alone. And some of those so-called caregivers are worse than alone. Mom would need an IV before they'd get off their butt to give her a drink.

So, our mothers live together and everyone is happy. Sure, Luisa is probably bored, but every couple of days she rearranges the furniture and they always walk down to the thrift stores and to Safeway.

"It's better than she had in Oaxaca," Elario says. He doesn't visit his mother much, but when he does and his eight speakers blast, Luisa thinks her son is a cruise missile coming down I-45. And she loves to wash his thick whitewalls with the counterspin hubcaps.

I can talk to Luisa because my Spanish is good in the present tense. Mom doesn't understand a word, but it's just as well. Luisa makes signs to her and squeals and laughs and mom seems to like it. Once they leave the apartment, Luisa never let's go of mom's hand. She's only about five feet tall, but she's got big arms and carries close to two hundred pounds.

When Carlos called to say that he was coming to say goodbye to his dad before he shipped out, Elario got all sappy. "When he was born, I told Marta we should name him Holiday Inn. Whenever she knew there was going to be an early checkout on her floor she'd call me and say, 'can you be here in ten minutes?' I was always there in five—I was only seventeen."

Elario asked me if he could use the store parking lot for the barbecue because he had no room at his apartment. "I'd be honored," I said, and I meant it. I was looking forward to meeting Carlos, the Marine.

"After he was born," Elario said, "I thought, Jesus, I'm gonna have fifty kids before I'm through, but you know what, he's the only one."

"You're not exactly out of business yet," I said.

"Everything is in the hands of God," he said.

And I sure found out how true that is when a guy who was talking on his cell phone rammed the side of my Chrysler going at

least forty. I lucked out in the accident, just broken ribs and a ruptured spleen in a totaled Chrysler. When I healed up, I decided that
I would do something to help others. I called Temple Beth Israel to
volunteer. I don't go much but I've been a member all my life. The
temple has a committee for just about everything—overweight teens,
mourners, singles under forty, over forty, interfaith, outreach.... I
narrowed it down to visiting the sick or temple maintenance, and
finally, I chose the sick over something like stacking chairs in the
audiovisual room.

After I sent in the paperwork, I got a welcoming call from
Assistant Rabbi Epstein. The office kept a list of sick members updated
daily, but he warned me to call first before going to visit a hospital
because they don't hold people like they used to. That I already knew.
I didn't tell him about my own hospitalization because I hadn't listed
any religious preference and I felt a little embarrassed by that when
talking to a rabbi.

The first sick person that the temple assigned to me was Morris
Fisher. The rabbi said he didn't know the man but he was in room
808 at Methodist hospital. Methodist, I've heard, is where the King
of Saudi Arabia stays when he comes to Texas. They keep a section
of one floor roped off for whenever he decides to use it, and for that
kind of service the King drops a few million a year on the hospital.
Maybe it's not true.

Anyway Mr. Fisher was in a regular room and when I knocked
and then came in he was half sitting up in bed, the game of solitaire
laid across his lap. He looked about seventy-five and there were no
tubes sticking out of him. I didn't know why he was in the hospital.
He held part of the deck in his hand. He didn't even say hello, he
just stared at me for a while, then he asked me to repeat my name.
"Aaron Evans," I said, and I gave him one of my business cards. "When
you're feeling better, stop by if you like auto accessories." His legs
twitched and there went his solitaire game all over the floor.

"Don't worry, I'll get the cards," I said, "it's been awhile since
I've seen anyone playing real solitaire now that every cell phone has
the electronic version." While I squatted under his bed I explained
that I was from the temple visiting committee.

"I didn't think it would be like this," he said, "I thought you would sneak in."

"I don't know what the rules are for the visiting committee," I said, "but why would I want to sneak in?"

I was already wishing that I had picked temple maintenance even before he asked, "are you allowed to talk about your mission?"

"We can talk about anything you want," I said, "baseball, cars, politics...."

He shook his head.

"I understand why you're here," he said, "maybe in the days of the Torah, visitors like you talked about sheep and goats."

I began to wonder if Mr. Fisher was a mental case even though Methodist isn't that kind of hospital. I told him again who I was and why I was visiting him.

"Beth Israel," he repeated the name of the temple slowly as if he was recalling it. "You've come to me from the house of Israel. That's good. He knows that I haven't always wanted to be there, but that's where I belong now."

I was glad to see him perking up a little.

"House of Israel," he said, "talk to me about the end of days, your specialty."

"My specialty," I told him, "is cars, what you probably call hot rods, you know, trim, special lowering kits, things like that. Modification."

"I've been ready since my wife died, we don't have to wait."

I was getting pretty uncomfortable, so I just asked him if we could watch TV and he said that was okay. I turned on the Astros game and made a few comments about Roger Clemens who was pitching, and I thought that if Mr. Fisher stopped talking nonsense, I might stay for an entire inning. And it seemed like he was watching the game too until he said, "let's not beat around the bush anymore, take me with you now and save everyone a lot of trouble."

I heard a nurse walking down the hall and as soon as she came in and strapped a blood pressure cuff on him, I shook his hand and said I had to go. He didn't let go of my hand.

"Do you know the date?" he asked.

"It's June 6th," I said, "I know it because it's D-Day."

"Do you have to visit again?" he asked.

"I could if you want me to," I said.

"It won't be necessary," he said, then he let go of my hand and I got out of there.

I pretty much knew what Mr. Fisher was getting at and that soured me on hospital visiting. I decided that in the future I would do my good deeds in some other, more cheerful way, maybe something with children.

I didn't forget about Fisher, I just decided not to think about what might have happened to him. Then, a month or so later, a man dressed in a suit and tie, which is unusual for our store, came in and asked for me. "He's a Fed or a collector," Elario said. Jacob Fisher was about forty, my own age, round faced with a fleshy nose. He gave me his card, a lawyer in some downtown office.

"I don't know if you remember visiting my father," he said.

I said that I remembered and right away I worried that maybe he'd come to sue me about something. I was trying to recall if I had actually touched his father and I was pretty sure that I hadn't laid a hand on the man except to shake hello and goodbye. "How's your dad?" I asked but I figured that the old gentleman was long gone.

"His health is good, in fact excellent," Jacob Fisher said, "although he doesn't believe it. He thinks that he has only a short time to live. In his mind he's made some kind of arrangement with God, and you, Aaron Evans are the messenger of doom, the stranger sent to him by God Almighty."

Elario who was listening, loved this. "Tell your papa that he's got the wrong man," Elario said, "*El Diablo* has the skull and crossbones seat covers and the antenna with the pirate flag."

Jacob Fisher looked at me as if calling for translation. "*El Diablo* is his car," I said, "the skulls, the snake, it's gang stuff. Most of them are really not bad guys, I do a lot of business with gangs. For them, Mr. Death is just their favorite dress up game; for some of them every day is Halloween."

"If we could get back to my father's situation," he said.

"I didn't bring up any of this with your dad," I said, "I just came in to say hello from temple."

"I understand," Jacob Fisher said, "dad's surgery was a hundred percent successful. He's seventy-three, not so old these days."

I agreed.

"But he has given up on life, he's ready to go. His house is all packed and labeled; he sold his car. He's a widower, my mother died four years ago. He says that September 6th is his date, exactly three months from the day of your visit."

"Well, on September seventh, his worries should be over," I said, "one way or another."

"I'm not able to joke about it," Jacob Fisher said, "the psychiatrist and I are afraid that he really might make it happen, the mind is a powerful thing—and I even worry about, God forbid, suicide."

I could see what a big thing this was for the son and I sympathized, because I know what it's like to have a parent who's in outer space.

"The reason that I'm here," he said, "is to ask your permission to bring dad for a visit to you. Maybe seeing that you own a store and are just a person will help him to snap out of it. The psychiatrist agrees that it's a good idea."

"It's okay with me," I said.

"I have offered to take dad to Florida, to Israel, anywhere. His answer is always the same, you can't escape Aaron Evans."

Elario burst out laughing. "I love it," he said, "we should print that on a bumper sticker." He made his voice creepy like a television commercial for a horror movie, "you can't escape Aaron Evans."

"Cut it," I said, "this isn't about playing tough guy in the neighborhood. Mr. Fisher believes that God sent me to him."

"The drugos all believe that too," Elario said. "I've seen guys in church so flooded that they can't stand up, but ask them about God and they'll tell you that they're the bleeding heart."

"Forget it," I said. I walked Jacob Fisher to his car, a dark blue Jaguar. I didn't even stock anything for a car like that, and I apologized for Elario. After meeting his son, that's when I really started to think a lot about Mr. Fisher. I didn't feel responsible for him, but his situation bothered me enough to call Rabbi Epstein, whom I shake hands with at high holidays, but I don't really know. I told him about my visit and asked about the angel of death stuff. I wanted to know if it was a Jewish thing.

"It's all superstition," he said, "there is no such character in Judaism. Of course there are stories. In every culture people personify death. When there's the unknowable or a man carrying a scythe and wearing a black hood, we prefer what we can see." He said that neither Morris Fisher nor his son had called him, but he would check in with them to see if he could be of any help. The rabbi wasn't surprised either, he had heard of such situations before. "Sometimes just being in the hospital brings on these encounters with mortality," he said. He advised me to forget about it, and maybe I would have if Elario hadn't started calling me Señor Muerte. Finally, I had to tell him that if he didn't stop, I would cancel the Carlos party, which I began to think might never happen because we hadn't heard from him again. Then he called one Thursday, to say that he'd be in on Sunday to say goodbye. With so little notice we had to hurry to get the party arranged. We have regular store hours, noon to seven on Sunday, so I posted a sign, 'Closing at 4 Sunday', and I called a mariachi band and ordered eight cases of beer and lots of barbecue and hot dogs. I told Elario that I would cover the expenses, "how many times am I going to have a chance to do something for a Marine," I said.

Just before the barbecue, I finally met Carlos. He was a skinny kid, maybe 130 pounds and about five foot ten. I had expected a big hulking Marine, more like Elario, who has a cannon sized beer gut, and Luisa who is a pure block. "A small mother," I thought.

I told Carlos to pick anything he wanted from the shop to decorate his tank or humvee or whatever the Marines used for transport, but all he picked was a set of mud flaps for a Honda. Then the barbecue problem came up. "I've been a vegetarian," Carlos said. "I started eating meat in basic because I had to, but I was thinking that this weekend, while I'm off, I'd like to get by on veggies."

"You hear that," Elario said, "he eats meat for his country. When did you start this vegetarian crap?"

"When I was a junior in high school," Carlos said, "didn't I ever tell you? Don't worry about it, I can buy a pack of veggie dogs, there's all kinds of them."

"You'll buy nothing," Elario said, "this is my party for you. French fries are okay though?"

"Perfect," Carlos said.

Elario had invited his buddies from the gang days, although I don't think he traveled with them that much anymore.

I closed the store at three-thirty to give Elario time to set up, then I went out to pick up supplies and later, Luisa and mom. When I got there the two of them were in a tug of war over mom's thermal jacket. Luisa was trying to pull it off her. "You're right," I told Luisa, "it's ninety-two degrees, but if she wants to wear a jacket, don't fight her." In the lobby, mom zipped her jacket as if to prove that she was right. Luisa had painted mom's fingernails bright red, and hers too. She was excited about seeing her grandson Carlos whom she had never met. She already had a grandson named Carlos in Oaxaca but that Carlos was just a baby.

I pulled up at the store with the ladies at about five-thirty. The fire was already going and there were a lot of people I recognized from the neighborhood. Then I spotted Morris Fisher and his son Jacob mingling in the crowd, each of them holding a longneck. The old man was wearing a *tallit*. I didn't mind him being there even if he thought it was a bar mitzvah, I just didn't want the old guy to go ballistic when he spotted me.

Luisa gave Carlos a bone crushing hug, only he wasn't Carlos. She had grabbed one of Elario's buddies and lifted him into the air. When she put him down he did the same to her. Carlos was over by the steel drum barbecue watching his veggie dogs to make sure they didn't get mixed in with the other ones. He wasn't in uniform, so I couldn't blame Luisa for not knowing which one was her grandson.

"Hi there," I said to Fisher and his son, "enjoy the party."

"Do you see?" Jacob said to his father, "It's all in your imagination. Aaron is a man, just like everyone else. He owns this store. You're standing in his parking lot." I gave the thumbs up to that.

Morris Fisher pointed to mom. "He's dragging the old lady away. Her time has come."

"She's my mother," I said, but it did look like I was dragging her along.

"September 6th," he said, "then it will be my turn."

"Stop it dad!" Jacob Fisher said. "This is a party, don't spoil it for Aaron."

He pointed to mom again. "She shouldn't be at a party, her party days are over."

Elario had finally gotten Luisa to the right person and she was hugging and picking up her grandson.

"Look at that," Elario called out to me. "Isn't that beautiful? The Marine and his grandma. Does anyone give a fuck if she's got a green card?"

Elario raised a long neck to make a toast. "For Carlos," he sang out, "my son the Marine. Stay safe and kick some ass over there."

Everybody cheered.

Carlos stood up on the bench and said, "thanks dad, and thank you everyone, but we're not going over there to kick ass. We're peacemakers, that's what Marines are all about."

Hector, one of Elario's buddies who came to the store now and then, grabbed Carlos from behind in a playful headlock. Like most of the men, Hector wore a leather vest over his bare chest, and he rubbed the marine's face against his graying chest hairs and the ornamental crosses that hung from his neck. "I'm a peacemaker too," he yelled, "get me into some action."

When the mariachi band started playing, Hector released the marine and Carlos took his grandmother by the hand and we all made a circle around them. Luisa could really dance. It surprised me how light on her feet she was. I wanted her to stay beside mom so that I could circulate but I didn't want to spoil her fun so I got mom a barbecue and settled her into a chair and made sure that she had a big wad of napkins.

"You okay?" I asked her.

"I'm hungry," she said.

I pointed to the sandwich right in front of her. "Eat," I said.

There were about forty or fifty people on the parking lot and a couple of good-looking women, but they were too fat, and anyway I wasn't about to strike up a conversation with someone else's woman, not in this crowd. When I had a chance, I moved over to say a few words to the Marine.

"You can't be too careful over there," I said.

"We're trained for exactly that," he said, "and Aaron, I want to thank you for giving my dad this job." He shook my hand. I felt like I was an uncle. When the marine left, Jacob came over to me. "I hope you don't mind that we're here," he said, "I thought that late Sunday would be a good time. We didn't intend to crash your party—and I couldn't stop him from wearing the *tallit*, it was the only way I could get him to come see you."

"Whatever it takes," I said. "Is he acting any better?"

"Worse," the son said. "He's canceled the electricity effective September fourteenth, he's giving us a week for shiva. He has nothing anymore; he's turned himself into a waiting room." Across the parking lot from us, Mr. Fisher stood. He didn't take his eyes off me. "The doctor told me to bring him here," Jacob said, "he advised me to do anything that would make dad active. Staying home and counting the days is the worst."

Elario was so drunk that I didn't know if he could tell Carlos from Morris Fisher when he brought the marine over to shake hands with the old man.

"Look at him," Elario said, "he's in uniform, and you're not." Elario had started drinking early, as soon as the beer arrived. The guy was flying and he had a woman hanging from his armpit. This was the first time I had seen Elario with his old crowd and I wasn't crazy about the way he was acting, but it was his party, his marine. I spent a little time with my mother and Luisa, and then I heard *el diablo's* pipes even before the crowd parted to make space for Elario on the lot. "The Marine has got to make his plane," Elario said. Carlos waved to everyone as he lowered himself into the front bucket seat.

"Grandpa," Elario yelled to Mr. Fisher, "have you ever been in a car that has a chandelier?"

"No," Morris Fisher said.

"Well, come on—*vamonos*—you're in for some thrills." The old man hesitated, but he did seem interested.

"I'm only going with Aaron Evans—are you going?" he asked me.

"No," I said. Even though I sold Elario and the rest of the crowd their kits and blocks, riding in their lowered cars made me feel like I was skateboarding on my back. Elario came over to help Mr. Fisher into the car. "You don't need Aaron," he said, "I'm your man."

"Tell dad to go," Jacob Fisher urged me, "it will be good for him."

Mr. Fisher waited for my approval and I knew that all I had to do was nod my head and he'd let Elario load him into the back seat. But even though he called me the angel of death, I sure didn't want him to get into Elario's car.

"You've still got some time," I said, "why not wait for me?"

"Okay," he said, "I'll wait." He turned away from Elario and walked to the only table on the lot. He sat down there next to my mother and Luisa who were still eating. Jacob Fisher ran at me, his fists clenched. "What's with you," he said, "you're playing right into his fantasy. I don't get it."

The Chevy backed slowly onto Fannin Street and then took off. At the freeway ramp, three inches above ground and with eight speakers blasting, Elario merged her onto I-10, aiming toward Baghdad. I walked over to the table, took my mother's hand and pulled her along. When Mr. Fisher asked if I wanted him too, I told him that he was more than welcome to come along for the ride.

Born in Grand Rapids, Michigan in 1941, MAX APPLE *has published two novels (*Zip *and* The Propheteers*), two story collections (*The Oranging of America *and* Free Agents*), and two memoirs (*Roommates *and* I Love Gootie*), as well as three screenplays and numerous essays and stories appearing in such places as the* Atlantic, Esquire, *and the* New York Times. *He has won* NEA, NEH, *and Guggenheim awards. Now living near Philadelphia, he teaches at the University of Pennsylvania.*

Steve Stern

The Ice Sage

1999

Sometime during his restless fifteenth year, Bernie Shtum discovered in his parents' food freezer—a white-enameled Kelvinator humming in its corner of the basement rumpus room—an old man frozen in a block of ice. He had been searching for meat, albeit not for the purpose of eating, though eating was Bernie's next to favorite pastime. But having recently sneaked his parents' copy of a famously scandalous novel of the Sixties in which the adolescent hero has relations with a piece of liver, Bernie was inspired to duplicate the feat. No stranger to touching himself, he hardly dared dream of touching another, so inaccessible seemed the flesh of young girls. His only intimacy so far had been with his mother's Hoover, innumerable pairs of socks, and his big sister's orchid pink underpants retrieved from the dirty clothes hamper in the bathroom. (This last item he kept hidden under his mattress, dragging them out at night to wrap around his chafed member or pull over his head to inhale the scent.) Then he'd come upon the novel he had once heard his parents sheepishly refer to as the required reading of their youth. Not a reader, Bernie had nevertheless browsed the more explicit passages, and so conceived the idea of defrosting a piece of liver.

Shoving aside rump roasts, Butterballs, and pork tenderloins in his quest, Bernie delved deeper among the frozen foods than he'd ever had occasion to search. Toward the bottom of the bin, once he'd emptied and removed the wire trays, the boy encountered a green-ish block of ice that stretched the length of the freezer. Scattering individually wrapped filets, tossing packages of French fries, niblets, and peas, Bernie was able to discern beneath the rippled surface of the ice the unmistakable shape of a man. It was an old man with a narrow, hawkish face, gouged cheeks, and a stringy yellow beard, his head wreathed in a hat like a lady's muff. His gaunt body was envel-oped in a papery black garment that extended to the knees, below which his sticklike calves, crossed at the ankles, were sheathed in white stockings. His feet were shod in buckled bluchers that curled at the toes, his arms folded behind his head as if he were taking a luxurious nap.

"Help!" cried Bernie, all prurient ambitions dispelled. Then convinced that he'd discovered something he shouldn't have, he bit his tongue and began rolling the boulders of meat back on top of the ice; he slammed shut the lid of the deep freeze, stumbled upstairs to his room, and crawled into bed where he tried to still his galloping heart. A solitary, petulant kid, chubby cheeks in their first flush of acne, Bernie was unaccustomed to any kind of galloping. But the next day he returned diffidently to the basement to determine if he'd seen what he'd seen, and that night at dinner, an ordinarily somber affair during which his father related his business woes to an indifferent wife, Bernie muttered, "There's an old man in the meat freezer."

"First chew, then swallow," replied his father. "Then speak." Proprietor of a prosperous home appliance showroom, Mr. Shtum looked askance at his son, who typically reserved a sullen silence dur-ing meals. Bernie repeated his declaration, still only barely audible.

Mr. Shtum pushed his horn-rimmed glasses back onto the hump of his nose and looked to his wife, who sat toying absently with her consommé. "What's he talking about?" he asked.

It took a moment for the fog to lift from her puffy face, eyes like bruises squinting from beneath a listing beehive. "Maybe he found the thing."

"The thing." Mr. Shtum's voice was level.

"You know, the white elephant."

"The wha—?" Mr. Shtum grew quiet, his hands beginning to worry the knot in his tie, whose tip skimmed his soup like a wick. "Oh, that."

"It's not an elephant," mumbled Bernie, "it's a man."

Mr. Shtum cleared his throat. "That's an expression, white elephant, like an heirloom. Some people have stuffed pets in the attic, or ceramic dwarfs; we got a frozen rabbi in the basement. It's a family tradition."

It had never occurred to Bernie that his family had any traditions.

Then it was his sister Madeline's turn to be heard from. A voluptuous girl excessively proud of her supernormal development, she condescended to inquire, "Like, um, what are you people talking about?"

Wary of his sister, who may have suspected him of stealing her underwear, Bernie slumped in his chair, avoiding her eyes. His father seemed to do likewise, for Madeline's radiance could be oppressive in their matte gray household; while Mrs. Shtum, still playing with her food, offered acerbically, "He's from your father's side of the family, they were always superstitious."

"He's a keepsake," Mr. Shtum was defensive, "handed down from generation to generation." Squaring his shoulders, trying to summon some pride for an object whose existence he'd clearly forgotten until now.

Annoyed, Madeline pushed her chair from the table, blew at a wisp of hennaed hair that fell instantly back into her eyes, and flounced out of the dining room. Moments later a shriek was heard from the basement, and Mr. Shtum made an uncomfortable face. "He came with a book, the rabbi," he said, as if the literature implied some official distinction. "Yetta, where's the book?"

"There was a book?"

Heaving a sigh, Mr. Shtum readjusted his glasses and got purposefully to his feet, departing the room just as Madeleine emerged from the basement, her robust complexion gone deathly pale. "I, like um, no longer want anything to do with this family?" she stated interrogatively.

"Here it is," announced Mr. Shtum, squeezing past his daughter to reenter the dining room. "It was in the bottom drawer of the dresser, under my Masonic apron." He was a joiner, Mr. Shtum, a member of local chapters of the Masons, the Lions, the Elks, with memberships dating from a time when Jews were not always welcome in such organizations. His prominence and civic-mindedness, however, had earned him the status of honorary gentile; he had even managed to secure his family a membership in an exclusive Memphis country club, which (with the exception of Madeline, whose endowments gave her entrée anywhere) the family seldom used.

Mr. Shtum handed a limp ledger book of the type in which accounts are kept to his son, who began idly thumbing the pages. Instead of figures, they were covered in an indecipherable script.

"The book explains where the rabbi came from," continued Mr. Shtum with authority. "My papa wrote it all down himself. The problem is, he wrote it in Yiddish." He may as well have said Martian. Then Mr. Shtum, a practical man of commerce, added apologetically, "He's supposed to bring luck."

Bernie took the ledger to his bedroom. Though his only enthusiasms to date had been a passion for overeating and his late penchant for erotic fantasy, he perused the scribbled pages intently. When the pages refused to give up one jot of their meaning, Bernie stuffed the book under his mattress alongside Madeline's panties and, for all his uncharacteristic excitement, fell promptly asleep.

1889–1890

When the holy man Rabbi Eliezer ben Zephyr, the Boibiczer Prodigy, wished to get closer to God, he would sit, or rather lie, by a certain pond in the woods outside his village. There, using techniques described in Gedaliah Ibn Yahya's *Girdle of Abimelech*, he would meditate on the letters of the Tetragrammaton until he entered a trance. In his youth he had been acclaimed for his public demonstrations of memory, his ability to recite passages of Talmud both forward and backward, and his feats of what the uninitiated called magic. But in his twilight years he was far beyond such exhibitions, and preferred to exercise his powers in solitude. He would lie upon his back on the mossy bank of the pond, his clasped hands cradling his head as the *Girdle* prescribed, while his soul ascended to the Upper Eden. There his soul sat in bliss among the archons studying Torah. Once, however, during one of his more intensive meditations—this was in the blustery month of Sivan just after Shavuot—there came a mighty storm. With his soul aloft, his body, frail as it was, remained insensible to the moods of the terrestrial world; and so, while the storm raged and the torrents battered his meager frame, Rabbi Eliezer continued his meditations in peace. The drenched earth on which he lay turned to mud and the water of the shallow pond began to rise, inundating his legs to the waist, creeping over his chest and chin and ultimately submerging his hoary head.

As their rebbe's retreats were routine, Eliezer's small band of disciples had grown accustomed to the old man's frequent absences. But that he should stay away so long in the wake of such a terrible storm, seemed to them a distinct cause for worry. After a couple of days, a party of Rabbi Eliezer's Chassidim, earlocks streaming, gabardines flapping like crows' wings, began combing the pastures and thickets known to be the tzaddik's special haunts. Deracinated trees with roots like hydras, the bloated carcasses of drowned hogs, and roofless peasant huts were what they found, but no Rabbi Eliezer. Some of his followers even passed in the vicinity of the pond that had overnight become a sizable body of water, underneath which lay the Prodigy in his mystical transports. (Previously he had depended on the *shulklapper* summoning the faithful to prayer to signal the reunification of his body and soul, but the deluge had muted any noises from above the surface of the lake.) When a week had passed without a rumor of their leader's whereabouts, the search was called off; the Chassids tore their garments, beat their pigeon breasts, and sprinkled ashes over their heads. They refused, however, to say Kaddish, as they contended one and all that their rebbe would one day return.

The seasons changed, the russet and gold autumn supplanted

by an alabaster winter, while Rabbi Eliezer continued his submarine meditations. The ground was blanketed, trees stooped like hunchbacks under duffels of heavy snow, and still the rebbe's body (completely immersed while his soul abided on high) remained impervious to decomposition. It was the time of year when the industrious widower Yosl King of Cholera, accompanied by his feckless son Salo, dragged his sledge across the snowfields to the banks of the Lower Bug to harvest ice. (He'd been an orphan, Yosl, whom the town had married off to another orphan during a plague in the hope of appeasing God's wrath—hence his name.) This year, however, Yosl had heard from the cheder boys who skated the horse pond on Baron Jagiello's estate that summer storms had increased the pond to the size of an inland sea. After investigating, Yosl went hat in hand to the Baron and begged permission to carve ice from his lake in exchange for replenishing the estate's own supply free of charge. An agreeable man when it served his interests, the Baron gave Yosl the go-ahead, and the ice mensch set out across the fields trailed by his son.

When they arrived at the swollen pond, there were a few truant Talmud Torah boys already there, their wooden skates describing wobbly arabesques on the surface of the jade-green ice. Abandoning his sledge, Yosl trod the ice in his hobnailed boots to test its thickness; then satisfied, began instantly to cut a trench with his axe. He called to his son to bring him the double-handled ice saw, but Salo, as timid as he was lazy, ventured only to the edge of the lake to hand his father the tool.

"*Amoretz!*" Yosl complained to the iron gray sky. "He puts his shoes on backwards and gets from walking into himself a bloody nose." But that was the extent of his indictment, since Yosl had long since abandoned any real expectations of his son. The boy's fear of almost everything in existence seemed to exempt him from life itself, let alone work, and sometimes his father wondered if Salo, whose mother had died in childbirth, had ever been entirely born.

While his father labored, Salo dawdled at the margin of the lake, ashamed as always to be hanging back but convinced that the ice would not support his lumpish weight. Occasionally, however, he might dare himself to rest the ball of a foot on the crusted surface, rubbing a circle as smooth as glass with the sole of his shoe. But rather than steal a glance through the polished porthole lest it reveal something untoward, Salo would turn quickly away. Though at one point he did catch sight, out the corner of an eye, of a fish like a butterfly wing suspended in a dark world where time stood still. And again, unable to resist a peek after he had rubbed another circle in the ice, he saw the face of an old man with a yellow beard.

"Papa!" Salo cried in terror.

In no particular hurry, Yosl trudged over to find out what his son was whining about this time. "*Gevalt*," he exclaimed upon seeing the thing the boy had accidentally revealed, "it's the rebbe!" Himself shaken to the core, Yosl slapped his own face to collect himself, then rounded up the other boys (his own was too slow) and dispatched them to the Chassids' study house with the news. The rebbe's disciples came running, some wearing only ritual vests and skullcaps despite the cold, arriving breathless to find that Yosl Cholera had already set about excavating their long lost leader. The ice mensch, his square jaw working like a whiskered feedbag, was dragging the rebbe, encased in a large block of ice, onto the shore of the lake with a grappling hook.

Then the Prodigy lay before them, and his gathered disciples, puffing vapor, were at a total loss as to what to do next. It was surely a blessing to have their tzaddik back in their midst again, intact even if frozen stiff, but what now? In former days it was the rebbe himself to whom they would have applied for advice, but the rebbe was unavailable for comment. There were the texts of holy writ of course, though even the most sedulous scholars among them—those who prescribed what portions of Torah one should consider during intercourse, or whether it was permitted to pee in the snow on Shabbos (which was tantamount to plowing, which was work and so forbidden)—even they knew of no passages pertaining to the current conundrum. Then one of their number, Zanvil Ostrov the yeast vendor, beard like a magpie's nest, proposed they light torches to thaw out the holy man on the spot. His theory was that Rabbi Eliezer, during his raptures, was proof against the depredations of time and the elements, and that once the ice was melted, he would be restored to them in all his prior vitality. There was thoughtful buzzing among them until a wiser head prevailed.

"Know-it-all," accused Berel Hogshead the teamster, insisting that such a proposal was preposterous, since, once thawed, the rebbe would rot and his bones, God forbid, become food for the worms. Better they should put him somewhere for safekeeping, so that at least he would remain in one piece until he chose to burst forth of his own accord. More buzzing in the affirmative as Yosl King of Cholera, neither Chassid nor Misnagid but simple opportunist, stepped forward in his capacity as proprietor of the Boibicz icehouse:

"Your honors, for a nominal fee—"

The Boibicz icehouse was a windowless granite grotto dug into the northern slope of a hill at the edge of the village by giants or fallen angels in some antediluvian age. That was the legend anyhow, which who but a Chassid believed? Yosl Cholera had inherited the icehouse after the death of Mendel Sfarb, its former proprietor, whose family claimed to have had it in their possession since the Babylonian Exile. The business was Mendel's guilty gift to the orphan who had been his ward and virtual slave. From outside, the sunken structure with its dome-like stone protrusion resembled an age-encrusted tomb, which made it the more suitable repository for the Boibiczer Prodigy; it was a place where his body could lie in state, so to speak, resistant to decay until such time as he saw fit to come forth again—or so his followers maintained. Much to Yosl's annoyance the Boibicz Chassidim insisted on honoring their rebbe's resting place as they would have a sacred sepulcher: they warbled their prayers (with the exception of the prayer for the dead) at its entrance, placed messages in the cracks between its stones, and took turns inside cleaning the sawdust and flax that collected around the holy man's transparent berth. Though they cautioned one another not to diminish its mass, they shaved discreet slivers from the block of ice, which they sweetened with dollops of honey and sucked. Since they never acknowledged the Prodigy as officially deceased, the Chassids were unable to appoint a successor, and thus came to be known for their veneration of the refrigerated rebbe as the Frozen Chassidim.

Diverting as were the antics of credulous fanatics, however, the inhabitants of Boibicz had other concerns to reckon with. *Ukases* were being issued by the imperial government in such dizzying succession that what was permitted in the morning was often forbidden by afternoon. The most recent stated that, for their own good, the Jews would be barred from leasing inns, taverns, and shops in the villages outside the Pale of Settlement. In addition, no new Jewish settlers would be allowed in the villages and hamlets within the Pale, which often included merchants returning from business trips or families from High Holiday worship in nearby towns. (The Byzantine logic of these laws defied the understanding of even the most learned Talmudists.) As a consequence, many longtime citizens of Boibicz had begun to find themselves homeless, and for those that remained the writing was on the wall. Eventually the Jews came to anticipate a wholesale exodus from a place that had been a home to their families for generations—in the face of which they dragged their heels. In the end it took a delegation of their neighbors, squired by a regiment of Cossacks dispatched by the government and operating under the blind eyes of the local police, to expedite their departure.

For all the chaos that erupted on that winter morning just after the Festival of Lights, the perpetrators went about their business almost mechanically, though the violence was no less savage for being deliberate. Without fanfare they entered the small Jewish quarter and smashed the shop windows, hauling out bolts of cloth, pedal-driven sewing machines, spirit lamps, unplucked chickens, anything that fell to hand. This included as well items for which they could have had no earthly use, such as spice boxes, menorahs, listless birds with split tongues in tarnished cages, phylacteries. They defecated in the synagogue vestibule and wiped their goose fleshed behinds with the torn vellum scrolls of the Torah. Feivush Good Value, *melammed* and tradesman, they hanged from his own shop sign by his patriarch's beard, then joked of the fine advertisement he made for his out-worn merchandise. They swung Shayke Tam, the idiot, by his heels, squealing because he thought it was all a game, until his feeble brains were splattered across the *shtibl* wall. They sliced open Frumeh Katz, discarded her unborn child and replaced it with feathers, then forced Moishe the tailor at bayonet point to stitch her belly back up. Those who fled to the woods were hunted down and beaten to splinters, though most who stayed put survived, among them Yosl Cholera's son Salo who'd taken refuge in the icehouse.

The fact was, he had scarcely strayed beyond the shadow of the icehouse since the day he'd stumbled upon Rabbi Eliezer ben Zephyr suspended beneath the surface of the lake. Though the frozen rebbe was scrupulously looked after by his followers, Salo had conceived the idea that the holy man was his own personal charge. He kept his ears pricked up for the stories the disciples told one another of the Boibiczer Prodigy's wondrous feats of piety, and when no one else was about, the boy (in age already a man) took his turn sitting vigil beside the block of ice. He admired the old man's tranquility while expecting, like his disciples, that at any moment the ice might crack open and the rebbe irrupt from his slumber. It was an event he had no desire to hasten, so pleasant was the waiting. To justify his hanging about the ice grotto, the boy made gestures toward helping his father, and Yosl, mistaking his son's efforts for a newfound interest in the business, encouraged Salo, who until now had shown interest in nothing on earth. But when the King of Cholera realized it was the frozen rebbe rather than the entrepreneurial impulse that had captivated his son, he wrote the boy off once again as a lost cause. Moreover, Salo's chronic attachment to the icehouse had been noted by his waggish peers, who gave him the nickname of Salo Frostbite.

So it was that, on the morning of the pogrom, Salo was seated on a cabbage crate gazing at Rabbi Eliezer's slightly distorted features, their beatific peacefulness having invaded his heart. All about him the stacked slabs of ice were carved into shelves and niches containing fish, fowl, and barrels of kvass. In one recess Leybl the hatmaker's dead dog Ashmodai awaited the spring thaw for its burial. Rime coated every jar and jeroboam until they looked like vessels made of spun sugar; ice stalactites hung from the vault of the ceiling like bared fangs. But the warmth Salo felt in the rebbe's presence, enhanced by his sheepskin parka whose collar he pulled over his ears, practically overwhelmed the arctic chill of the grotto in its subaqueous light, a light that seemed to emanate from the ice itself. Never having shown the least affinity for spiritual matters—he'd been drummed out of cheder by an exasperated teacher for congenital obtuseness—Salo stole into the icehouse to sit beside the rebbe whenever his followers left him unattended; and more and more, as the disciples too fell prey to evictions and hopelessness, they left their tzaddik alone.

"While the Chassidim sit shiva, you sit and shiver," Salo's father had complained, but in the rebbe's presence all the chimeras of the boy's fearful imagination were dispelled, and the world seemed almost an idyll, a winter pastoral. As a consequence, Salo never heard the cries of the tortured and defiled, the keening women and the breaking glass, nor did he smell the smoke from the burning synagogue. It was only when the sexton Itche Beilah Peyse's, who'd lost his mind, began to howl like a hyena in the street, that Salo's own peace was finally unsettled.

Bestirring his broad behind, he crawled up the slippery ramp and wriggled out of the hatch through which Yosl slid his rectangular ice cakes into the grotto. He stumbled down the hill into the village, past the shabbos boundary markers where the snow was stained in patches with what appeared to be plum preserves. Outside the door of the smoldering timber synagogue a mother tried to revive her fallen son by pumping air into his lungs with a pair of bellows; a violated daughter begged her father on her knees in the rutted market platz not to disown her. The procession of wagons hauling bodies already gone stiff to the cemetery vied with the jauntier parade of peasants carrying off samovars, chamber pots, a trumpet-speakered phonograph, a cuckoo clock. Plodding forward in his clunky boots, Salo accidentally toppled the cantor Shikl Bendover, who had died of fright still standing like Lot's wife. He paused to re-erect the dead man then realized what he was about to do, and understood that the scene he had entered trumped any his active fancies might invite. It put to rest forever the inclination toward nightmarish invention, for which Salo, who began suddenly to outgrow himself, was grateful.

He stepped into the smoky slat-shingled hut that he and his father called home, where he discovered that he'd been made an orphan like his father before him. Yosl King of Cholera lay on the raked clay floor in the stiff leather apron he'd donned for work, his head pincered by his own ice tongs. The handles of the iron tongs curled above his crimped skull like antlers, the blood streaming in crimson ribbons from his ears. Salo retched down his front and fell to his knees, leaning forward to touch those of his father's features that were still recognizable: a blue knuckle swollen from arthritis, a pooched lower lip like a water leech. For an hour or two he lay prostrated without the least impulse ever to rise again; until he remembered that he now had a higher calling. Wiping his mouth and dabbing at his eyes with his sleeve, Salo got to his feet and began rummaging in the debris of the ransacked hovel, eventually locating a pair of candles. These he lit with a sulfur-tipped match and placed at either end of his murdered father's outstretched form, all the while murmuring Kaddish. He threw a cloth over the mirror, its surface clouded with floes of mercury. Then he squeezed himself behind the cold tile stove and pried loose a wallboard, in back of which his father had hidden his meager treasures—a handful of groschen, some ducats as worthless as slugs, an unsigned postcard with a sepia view of Lodz, a thimble that had belonged to his wife. Salo thrust it all into a deep pocket along with a crust of black bread and some dried herring already gnawed by mice. He emerged from the cottage just as Casimir, a sooty-eyed Polish porter with hair like burnt thatch, was dragging along Yosl's pussle-gutted mare by a frayed piece of rope; and though he knew the beast to be next to useless, Salo straightaway turned over his inheritance (minus the postcard and thimble) to the porter in exchange for redeeming the skewbald nag.

He was aware, of course, that Rabbi Eliezer ben Zephyr, if he belonged to anyone, belonged to his worshipful followers. But the Frozen Chassidim and their families were packing up their belongings along with everyone else, and nowhere amid that doleful exodus of clattering barrows and carts heaped high with candlesticks and featherbeds did Salo spy any monumental block of ice. Ingenuity had never been his strong suit; indeed Salo had never had a strong suit, but drawing from a fund of proficiency that he decided was his father's bequest to his son, he undertook to replace the metal-rimmed wheel on Yosl's delivery wagon. When he'd managed over the course of an onerous hour to unhobble the wagon, he hitched it to Bathsheba the mare, whose sluggish forward propulsion seemed entirely owing to her chronic flatulence. Salo stopped at the *beis hamidrash* long enough to reclaim the cedar casket that leaned against an interior wall beneath the half-collapsed roof. This was the single battered casket (overlooked during the afternoon's mass burials) that the village had recycled for the funerals of the past hundred years. Loading it onto the wagon, the youth continued leading the horse up the hill to the icehouse, where he studiously addressed the heavy mechanism of a block and tackle. He proceeded to snake the pullied device through the hatch down into the stygian grotto, like lowering a bucket into a well, then lowered himself for the purpose of attaching the cables to the ice. Back outside, awakening muscles that had slumbered the greater part of his sixteen years, Salo hauled the rebbe by main force up the wooden ramp into the failing light of day. Then, sweating profusely despite the bitter cold, he slid the block of ice up a second makeshift ramp of sagging planks into the bed of the wagon. There he began chipping at the edges of the ice with his father's axe until he could shove the block, wrapped in burlap for further insulation, through the hinged panel at one end of the casket. Since Bathsheba's belly dragged the ground as if she had fed on cannonballs, there was no question of mounting the wagon, so Salo tugged at the reins and set off walking without further delay—as who was there left to say goodbye to?—in the general direction of the city of Lodz, which lay beyond the Russian Pale.

1999

Finding an old Jew in the deep freeze did not at first alter Bernie Shtum's routine in any measurable way. Overweight and unadventurous, he had no real friends to tell the story to, even if he'd wanted, which he did not: it was nobody's business. But even Bernie had to admit to himself that something had changed. It was still late summer and he continued, as was his custom, to spend most of each day in front of the TV, munching malted milk balls and digging at his crotch. Images passed before his eyes without leaving distinct impressions: In a comic sketch a failed suicide bomber was comforted by his veiled mother to gales of canned laughter; in another a little girl kept God in her closet; a heartwarming Hallmark drama portrayed a Navy SEAL romancing a mermaid. A reality-based program dispatched a disabled couple on a blind-date to Disneyworld, and in another an ordinary family volunteered to spend a year in an igloo. There were elections, massacres, celebrity breakups, corporate meltdowns—all of which tended to evaporate upon entering Bernie's mind. Still, he remained a passive captive of the flickering tube in the faux-paneled basement, which was largely his private domain. (His father's was the upstairs den, his mother's the bedroom in which she cat-napped over novels with embossed titles.) The only new wrinkle in the fabric of his days was that, while surfing the myriad channels, Bernie would also idly fan the pages of the ledger book, the one in which his grandfather had chronicled the history of the frozen rabbi. And periodically he would rise and shuffle over to the freezer, where he rolled aside the packaged ground round and game hens to make certain that the old man was still there.

Then came the weekend his parents had gone to Las Vegas, all expenses paid, for a home appliance convention. They naturally had no problem with leaving the adolescent Bernie alone, since the boy had never demonstrated the least propensity for mischief, and at nineteen the headstrong Madeline, on vacation from college, would do as she pleased. It was Friday night around eight o'clock when the storm hit, one of those semi-tropical electrical storms with typhoon-force winds that often swept through Bernie's southern city in August. The television reported that funnel clouds had been spotted around the perimeter of the city, their tails corkscrewing the ground like augers, sundering mobile homes. Lightning crackled and thunder sounded like kettledrums, rain hammered the roof of the two-story colonial house, while Bernie sat more or less oblivious on the rumpus room sofa. It wasn't that he was without fear so much as that primary events had no more impact on the boy than events (give or take the odd brassiere commercial) on TV.

There was a violent Götterdämmerung of an explosion, after which the lights went out and the image on the TV shrank to a dot, then disappeared. Bernie continued sitting alone in the windowless dark clutching the ledger, as what else was there to do? His sister was out with one of her boyfriends, not that her puffed up company would have been much consolation; so there was nothing for it but to sit listening to the wind like a droning propeller and waiting for the floodwaters to rise above the roof of the house. When, after an indeterminate time, the storm began to abate, the boy was almost disappointed. The power, however, had still not come back on, and in the wake of the squall he could hear the sound of a hollow knocking nearby. He lifted himself from the sofa's recessed cushions and groped his way to the shelves that housed the overflow of his father's framed civic citations. Perspiring freely since the cessation of the central air, Bernie stooped to open a cabinet beneath the shelves, foraging blindly among dusty wine bottles and photograph albums until he located the plastic handle of a flashlight. He switched it on and aimed its beam toward the source of the thumping.

Standing over the freezer cabinet, Bernie slowly lifted the chromium handle that released the lid. Instantly the lid flew open, soggy steaks and tenderloins sliding onto the floor, as up sat a sodden old man like an antiquated jack-in-the-box, his fur hat stinking like road kill. There was a moment when the old man and the boy with his gaping jaw seemed transfixed by one another; then the old man's scarlet eye grew narrow and gimlet-sharp, and shaking himself, he asked in a rusty voice, *"Iz dos mein aroyn?"*

Even had he been able, Bernie would not have known how to respond.

Groaning and soaked to the skin, his hands and face the consistency of wet papier mâché, the old man endeavored to rise, only to fall back splashing into the freezer. *"Dos iz efsher gan eydn?"*

Again Bernie, his heart rattling the cage of his ribs, could only shake his head.

"A glomp," said the rabbi decisively, *"a chochem fun Chelm,"* as he held out his scrawny arms for the boy to help him up. Bernie remained immobile with awe, but as the old man's anticipation had an air of authority, he took an involuntary step forward. The rabbi was no more than a featherweight, but his saturated ritual garments hung on him heavily, and, in attempting to lift him, Bernie felt as if he were involved in a wrestling match. When he'd managed to drag

the old man from his sloshing sarcophagus, his crumbling garments clinging to his body like bits of eggshell to a fledgling bird, both the boy and the elder tumbled together onto the apple green carpet. Just then the lights came back on, the TV blaring, its screen displaying a smug emcee making a face as contestants swallowed the placentas of voles. The defrosted rabbi, sprawled atop Bernie who had yet to release him, squinted with interest at the show.

"*Voo bin ikh?*" he inquired.

At that moment, leading her escort in his crested blazer by the hand down the basement stairs, Bernie's sister spied the half-naked old party in the process of extricating himself from her brother's embrace, and screamed bloody murder.

STEVE STERN *is the author of several works of fiction, including* Lazar Malkin Enters Heaven, *which won the Edward Lewis Wallant Award for Jewish American fiction, and* The Wedding Jester, *which won the National Jewish Book Award. He teaches at Skidmore College and will be a Fulbright Fellow at Bar Ilan University in the fall of 2004.* "The Ice Sage" *is part of a work in progress.*

Aryeh Lev Stollman

Bring Me into Paradise

A good child redeems his parents from
Gehinnom and even brings them into Paradise.
—Gaon of Vilna

Whenever she was visiting from Toronto, Grandma always managed to say the same things, especially if lady company was over and Mother went into the kitchen to make tea and cut up cake.

"Who'd have dreamed my own daughter, my own flesh and blood, would marry a rabbi and move to this cow town!"

My mother, rolling her eyes and smiling at the company, would enter the living room with the tea tray or cake platter in her hands. "For the millionth time, Ma, there are no cows in Windsor."

"For the millionth time, Sarah," Grandma would say, staring so hard at the ladies that they'd twist in their seats, "for the millionth time, I don't know who the bigger moron is, you or your sister Helena."

Meanwhile Aunt Helena, who wouldn't notice if a bomb exploded in front of her, would be sitting in the corner watching the television screen without the sound on.

Then Mrs. Seabert, one of the ladies, would say, "Really Nora, you shouldn't complain, you're lucky to have a son-in-law like our rabbi."

"Seabert, I wasn't complaining. I was just discussing facts."

Then Grandma would go on how she worried because her grandchildren, and there were bound to be plenty of them under the circumstances, would be religious fanatics, and cave people, and worst of all hicks.

"Look at Alexander, the little shrimp looks like a rabbi already!"

"Ma!" my mother would say in my defense.

The fact is Grandma was wrong, lying actually, about having plenty of grandchildren. Everyone knew, and so did she, that my mother's womb was booby-trapped. She had had to stay in bed for three months before I was born because I almost fell out before I was ready. I even had an older brother who I never knew because he fell out too soon and died. Mother said he was small as a pear and had tiny hands and feet. "It's too bad," she said. "It would have been nice for you to have an older brother."

Sometimes I dream I do have an older brother who is smart and tall and handsome and takes me everywhere with him. Sometimes in my dreams we ride our bikes so fast that soon we are flying over our house and up Victoria Avenue. And then when I awake, I'm mixed up and sad and remember that really I don't have a brother. Once I told my friend Meyer I had an older brother who died but he said it didn't count if he was born dead. "Lots of people have one of those."

Anyway, I was, and still am, Grandma's only grandchild. My father said in a sermon that people have mental blocks and even forget things on purpose, especially when it comes to things God wants them to do. Grandma says she doesn't believe in rabbis except for my father because he is tall and handsome and doesn't make my mother wear a wig like the fanatic rabbis.

Before Aunt Helena suddenly died, Grandma and Aunt Helena lived in Toronto in a neighborhood that, as far as I could tell, looked just like Windsor.

"Take care you don't fall too deep," Grandma would say if Mother made me call to read her my report card and I got to the part about the A's in Bible and Talmud. "Take care you don't fall for that nonsense or you'll drown."

Sometimes I visited Grandma in Toronto for a few days. In

Windsor, with my parents around, Grandma hardly talked directly to me but in Toronto it was different and she told me all sorts of things.

"You know Alexander, I don't believe in all that hocus-pocus your parents and school are brainwashing you with. I don't believe in that God-watching-over-the-world business and do you know why?"

I never said yes or no because I knew what she would say, I had heard it so many times before. "Do you know why?" she'd repeat, pointing at Aunt Helena, who sat sleeping in a chair wearing some brightly colored dress. "Exhibit A. I rest my case."

When Aunt Helena, who was one year younger than my mother, was a little girl, she was very smart but then she caught a brain fever. Everyone thought she would die but she didn't, only she turned retarded. Grandma said that if they had figured it out a few days earlier, maybe she wouldn't have gone retarded. Grandma said Grandpa died a few months later because he couldn't face facts.

"Where was this God of yours when Helena went retarded?" Grandma always asked me as if it were my fault.

I never said anything when Grandma started in on God and Aunt Helena, even though I read *Youth Rejoice,* which is the book I won at school when I learned six chapters of Genesis by heart. My teacher Rabbi Flucht said it was a great book because it had the answers to all the difficult questions young people are always asking. I read in *Youth Rejoice* that sometimes things happen that seem bad but turn out to be good, like when you stand too close to a painting and see an ugly black streak and then step back and see it's really the edge of a beautiful tree or a wonderful bird.

I also read in *Youth Rejoice* that retarded people and insane people and children who are kidnapped and raised by wicked people go directly to Paradise in the World-to-Come because they don't have free will so they don't have any sins. And the other thing is, even if terrible things happen to you in this world, God can make it up to you in the next and everything that happened bad to you in this world is only like a dream. "Oh, I had a bad dream," you might say when you finally go to Heaven.

Once, I told Grandma that maybe in Paradise God would make it up to Helena, and she'd be a genius.

"Sounds like you're retarded," she said.

Usually when I went to visit Grandma in Toronto she would take me to the Science Center or to Casa Loma or a movie and we'd leave Aunt Helena at home. "It's all right. She can be alone for a few hours," Grandma said. Sometimes though, Grandma and I went shopping with Aunt Helena, which was very boring. Grandma said that Helena needed beautiful clothes to show the world she's an important person too. I would be bored because Grandma would go with Aunt Helena into the dressing room and it would take forever until they came out with Aunt Helena wearing another bright red or blue dress. Then the salesladies would fuss and pin things and take down measurements. Once Grandma asked my opinion of a red dress Helena tried on and I accidentally told the truth and said, "She looks like a tomato," because she was also pretty fat.

"Don't make fun of your Aunt Helena," Grandma screamed in front of all the salesladies.

"But you call her moron!"

"When you decide to take care of her the rest of your life you can call her a moron too!"

Later, on the telephone, Grandma told my mother, specially loud so I would hear, "That little rabbi of yours is gonna be trouble one day."

Grandma once told me if Helena hadn't gone retarded she'd be more beautiful than my mother. "I'm not knocking your mother, she's my daughter too, but Helena was always prettier when they were little. Everyone said, 'Sarah's pretty but that Helena's a real beauty.'"

Grandma said, even though Helena is fat now and my mother isn't, they look a lot alike and have the same fine nose and wavy black hair.

After that I started having a certain nightmare. Sometimes I'll be running away from a dog or a monster and I'll come running to the screen door of the kitchen because that's where my mother is. Instead, when I get there, Aunt Helena's standing behind the door and she's too stupid to let me in. Then in the dream I get mixed up and I'm not sure if it's Aunt Helena or my mother or both. I don't know what happens after that because that's when I wake up.

Father always says we mustn't judge Grandma even though she doesn't believe in anything because she suffered so much. "Having a retarded child is worse than cancer," my father says. My father also says everyone is responsible for everyone else and it works both ways. If we make someone do something wrong it's like we did it ourselves because you're not supposed to put a stumbling block before the blind. And if we cause someone to do good we get credit for the good deed as well. My father says if we are any good it's partly to Grandma's credit because she raised my mother. "If we get to go to Heaven, Grandma comes with us."

I also read in *Youth Rejoice* that if your parents are wicked you can bring them into Paradise by doing good deeds which is sort of what my father says.

Whenever Grandma and Aunt Helena would visit us in Windsor, Mother always offered to care for Helena so Grandma could go away on vacation.

"Ma, I'm perfectly capable of caring for my sister without you around. Why don't you go to Florida?"

"You'll have plenty of time to care for Helena when I'm dead. Then I'll go to Florida!"

Mother said that having Helena was no problem because she could feed herself and even dress herself if you helped her a little. Mother said Helena was gentle as a lamb, which was true, and a perfect angel, which wasn't. If Mother couldn't find the pearl necklace that Father gave her when I was born or her favorite blue Aynsley teacup with gilt edges was missing from the china cabinet she would quietly search the guest room where Aunt Helena and Grandma slept and find the missing object in a dresser drawer or under the bed or in one of the suitcases in the closet. Once she found the silver and crystal toothpick holder in Aunt Helena's pillowcase.

If I caught Mother snooping around the guest room, she would turn around guiltily as if she herself were a thief. "Aunt Helena forgets to ask when she wants to borrow something," Mother would say, as if I were retarded.

Once Mother bought some shiny fake jewelry at Woolco for an experiment and put it on the buffet table but Helena never took it. "Helena's smarter than you think!" Grandma said.

Whenever Grandma wanted Mother to take her to Shanfield's or Birk's to buy those Wedgwood dishes with Queen Elizabeth II or a maple leaf in the center, she would leave Helena at the house. "We're liable to be arrested."

Although she was always complaining about God and religion, Grandma acted like a brown-nose with my father. Whenever he came into the kitchen or dining room, Grandma would pop out of her chair like Rebecca in the Bible. "Can I get you something to drink, dear? Would you like some tea or coffee?" and because everyone knows it's a big production for Grandma just to turn on the stove, my father would usually say, "No thanks, Ma. I'm in a hurry," and grab a bottle of Verners from the refrigerator and go off to his office to prepare a sermon or visit someone in the hospital. Even Aunt Helena, who wouldn't notice if you were hit by a car right in front of her, would follow my father around the room with her eyes and make funny snorting noises.

"All the women in this family have the same taste," Grandma would say.

Even though she said she didn't believe in it, Grandma would go to synagogue on Saturday mornings whenever she was in Windsor. "I'll make a cameo appearance. I don't want those idiots talking bad about the rabbi's mother-in-law." Grandma, Mother and Aunt Helena wore wide-brimmed hats with flowers or feathers when they went to synagogue. Grandma always bought Aunt Helena the most elaborate hat of all, sometimes with tall ostrich feathers or birds-of-paradise, because she didn't want Helena outdone by all those "fancy fakers." They would all leave the house in time for my father's sermon and flutter up Giles Boulevard like strange and wonderful birds. In synagogue Grandma sat silently between her daughters while everyone was singing and she wouldn't even move her lips to say amen. Usually she wouldn't talk to her friends like Mrs. Seabert or Mrs. Rosenthal while she was still in the synagogue. "They're all hypocrites," she said, "they only come to services to talk and gossip."

But if Mother invited the same ladies over to the house for afternoon tea, Grandma would start talking to them again and go on and on how her daughter married a rabbi or how much she missed Toronto or how Windsor was such a cow town until once Mrs. Rosenthal said, "Nora darling, are you referring to us?"

"God forbid, Esther. I would never insult the cows."

Mother said she worried we'd be run out of town one day on account of the things Grandma said. Father said she shouldn't worry or be hard on Grandma, because of all she suffered. Mother told me, "Your Father always looks on the good side of people, which is part of the reason I married him, but sometimes I think he might be crazy."

"It's unnatural," Grandma was telling my mother in the kitchen as if I couldn't hear her in the dining room where I was doing my homework. "It's abnormal for a ten-year old child to start looking more and more like an old rabbi."

"Alexander is almost twelve," my mother said.

"Well, he looks like ten. I hope he's not turning into a dwarf!"

"Ma!"

"Well, it's unnatural running around all the time with a Stetson. It's because you send him to that horrible school."

"Ma, it's a perfectly good school. It's only a custom. If Alexander wants to wear a hat he can wear a hat. It's a free country."

Just then Aunt Helena came creeping down the stairs like a zombie in the pink muumuu Mrs. Seabert brought her from Hawaii. I told my friend Meyer that my Aunt Helena had special moron radar even though she didn't hear too well, and would wake up and come downstairs whenever Grandma and Mother were arguing.

"Look, Sarah. You woke Helena," Grandma said.

Grandma as usual was exaggerating because I didn't run around "all the time" wearing my hat, which wasn't even a Stetson. I only wore it when I went to school or to synagogue. I never wore it in the house or when I went playing or shopping or anything. I go to Solomon Day School in Detroit, which is across the river from Windsor since there is no day school in Windsor. All the older boys at Solomon wear hats when they turn thirteen because that's when they're supposed to be like adults. Since I skipped a grade (Rabbi Flucht says I'm a cistern that doesn't lose a drop) I'm younger than everyone else and I didn't want to be the only one in class who didn't wear a hat.

"You have plenty of time to throw away your life," Grandma said when she passed me in the dining room while taking Helena back upstairs.

I didn't answer back even though it says in *Chapters of the Fathers* that you should know how to answer the scoffers and learn their way of thinking, even if it's a bad influence, so you can tell them off. I wasn't even wearing my hat while I was doing my homework and Grandma started all her complaining.

Grandma's also a hypocrite because my father wears a hat when he goes to synagogue and once I head Grandma say, "That's a very fine hat, dear."

The main reason I started wearing a hat to school even though I wasn't thirteen yet and didn't have to, was that lots of boys in my class acted as if I came from Mars. A lot of them had never been to Windsor and if I would mention that I lived in Canada which is a foreign country like China or France or Israel, Martin Hoffstader would say, "You speak English so you must live in America, or are you a little Martian?" And I'd say, "I don't know who the bigger moron is, you or my Aunt Helena." It was bad enough that I was younger than anyone in class and had to deal with morons, I didn't want to be the only one who didn't wear a hat.

"You think there are no more surprises," Grandma always says when she's about to tell how Aunt Helena suddenly died. I've heard her tell the story so many times now it seems I've seen it all on television.

"Helena got out of her chair and opened her mouth like she was finally going to speak after almost thirty years. I thought maybe there really are miracles and she's coming out of her retardation so I rushed over to her. I said, 'Sweetheart, talk to me' and I held her in my arms and didn't even realize for a moment that she dropped dead in my arms, which is why she suddenly turned heavy and fell back into her chair."

If company is over and one of the ladies says, "How terrible!" Grandma says, "My daughter died and you're telling me it's terrible?"

Later Dr. Lear told Grandma that maybe Aunt Helena had a heart attack and maybe something was wrong with her heart from when she became sick and went retarded. Dr. Lear said that maybe Helena's death was a blessing in disguise.

"*Your* death would be a blessing," Grandma told him.

Grandma had Helena buried in Windsor even though she died in Toronto. "She should be near her sister; who knows how long I'm going to last."

The first time I heard Grandma tell the story of how Helena suddenly died was in our kitchen the night before the funeral. While Grandma was talking, Mother was boiling water for tea and even Father was in the kitchen listening to Grandma. The kettle started steaming and that's why whenever I think of Helena dying, I think of steam and I see her soul coming out of her mouth like vapor, only it doesn't make any noise and disappears into the air.

That night, before we went to bed, Grandma said she didn't want to sleep alone and she didn't want Mother to sleep with her either because she should cleave to her husband like it says in the Bible.

"Maybe Alexander can sleep in the room with me, if it's not against his religion." So I slept on a cot in my room and Grandma slept in my bed. Mother didn't want me to sleep in the guest-room with Grandma. Even though she generally isn't superstitious, the idea of my sleeping in the same room where Helena used to sleep gave her the heebie-jeebies.

In the middle of the night I woke and saw Grandma get out of bed and walk over to the window that looks out over our front lawn. The moonlight coming in turned her nightgown see-through so I didn't look for more than a second because I could see her droopy bosoms hanging down under her nightgown like the fox stole she wore when she dressed up. I pretended I was asleep but she came over to my cot and tapped me on the shoulder. "Alexander...do you know what I dreamed? I dreamed I bought Helena a beautiful new hat and I said, 'Sweetheart do you like your new hat?' Not that I expected her to answer but she said as if it was perfectly natural for her to talk, 'Can I wear it in Heaven?' and then she looked just like she did when she was a little girl, before she got sick, and I cried in my dream because she was so beautiful."

Grandma stood quietly by my cot for a while and I didn't say anything because I didn't know what to say. At first I kept thinking that maybe I breathed in Aunt Helena's soul from the tea kettle and maybe I would have retarded children and then I remembered that's what I was dreaming before I woke up and heard Grandma getting out of bed.

I think dreams must be contagious because when I fell asleep again, I dreamed Aunt Helena was standing by my cot in one of her hats with enormous feathers and flowers. I wasn't really sure if it was my Aunt Helena or my mother or maybe even Grandma. She kept opening and closing her mouth but no words came out.

I read in *Youth Rejoice* that every dream has a kernel of truth and I also read that when the Temple was destroyed, God took the gift of prophecy away from the prophets and gave it to children and imbeciles and I thought maybe Helena would become a moron prophetess who came to you in dreams.

Lots of people came to the funeral because my mother is the rabbi's wife and Aunt Helena was her sister. When we came into the crowded chapel Grandma said, "People love a tragedy." Everyone was crying when my father gave the eulogy. Mother says Father has a golden tongue and knows how to raise people out of their selfishness. Father said Helena had a pure and simple soul and it was from Helena and my grandmother that he understood the mystery of Love, which brings us into Paradise. After all, my father said, Paradise is not a mere physical place but the beauty and light of God's eternal love. When he said that I turned to look at Grandma and my mother. Mother was crying, but Grandma just said, "I'll believe it when I see it."

I read in *Youth Rejoice* that nobody in this world can imagine the joys and beauty of the World-to-Come, which is a great mystery of God's Being. We are like the man, blind from birth, standing in front of a great palace, who cannot see or know the beautiful building or the wonderful gardens. But there is one thing we can know and be sure of; when our eyes are made to see and we are brought into Paradise, we'll be glad we are there.

ARYEH LEV STOLLMAN, *a neuroradiologist, is the author of two award-winning novels,* The Far Euphrates *and* The Illuminated Soul, *and a collection of stories,* The Dialogues of Time and Entropy. *His work has been translated into five languages. "Bring Me Into Paradise" was his first published story and appeared in an earlier form in the magazine* Stories *(1988).*

v. Verse

Gerald Stern

L'chaim and Other Poems

There goes that toast again, four stinking
glasses full of some kind of ruby held up
to the sun this time, death crumbs falling and rising
like dust-motes, fish eggs, bubbles, here's to you, bubbles,
here's to Mardi Gras, here's to the apple tree
pinned against my fence, here's to reproach,
here's to doing it to music, here's to fog,
and here's to fog again, and life dividing
inside the fog; oh when it dissipates
let's make a circle; here's to the baby hiding
inside his clothes, here's to his being
alive without me, here's to the mountain again
for what the hell, I might as well be on the mountain,
here's to delectables, free health care, love, popcorn.

Maggid

DESNOS[1]

Regards To Bill Kulik

I considered the bourgeois virtues for one day
and it was my birthday when on a Wednesday morning
the palmist who walked among the corpses in Buchenwald
was sent on his journey by the Gestapo in Paris,
he, the official dreamer of WXYZ,
he, the friend of Chico Marx and Bert Williams;
so much for thrift, hard work, piety and patriotism,
so much for spending the principal and for the argument
against gratification and the argument for, and guess
how the light shone on my grandfather's stick and guess
if it was a marigold he carried in his hairy mouth.

CITY OF GOD

It takes longer now than it used to take
and I am tempted to climb the back stairs
which have two risers less than the front ones and
it comes to thirteen rather than coming to fifteen
though they are curved, which adds a lateral motion
to the blood-starved thigh, making up in cunning
what it lacks in slope and there at the top
instead of a bald and flaking mirror you almost
walk inside of, a book that you trip over,
The City of God, him and a snake on the cover
staring at each other, the snake with an eye
that's mostly film, the saint's half-crossed, the two
are so close together, and they are arguing
about my future, and one of them is a prick,
outside my bedroom, down the sloping hallway.

* Robert Desnos, the great French poet, calmed his fellow prisoners at Buchenwald
  by reading their palms.—GS

GOLDEN RULE

All he wants is for you to stay away from his egg
and all he wants is for you to shut up when it comes
to the three things he hates the most, justice,
mercy, humility. He detests Jesus and he can define
what he is, and was, and wants to be while flying
unbearably low by the one word, squack, and
that is why I pulled my straw hat down over
my bald head and that is why my orange cat
almost died with fear and why he, why *he*, won
the argument with his big black shadow while resting
              only on one leg.

THE TASTE OF DUCKLINGS

That's the stick I made a marsh for and leaned
two rocks against, the one that lived through snow
and cat piss and dish towels, and those are the neighbors I hate
though I love their dog and that is the sky I brought into
my kitchen, including the clouds, and the turtle that loves
the taste of ducklings, he swims under water, and that is
the bush that hides everything there against the
chain-link fence, the thing I loved dragged through
the mud, though mud is just dirt and water
and nothing more—just try ascribing a soul
to water and dirt, just try blowing your meat-filled
breath on what your hands made, bomb-crazed lunatic.

SOUP

After he left I turned to my cold soup
for I was starving after so much talk,
and as a precaution I pulled the blind down and took

the phone off the hook, and I was using a spoon
that had to belong to an earl once, a pink
pig he had to be, for there was a spot of
pink in the heraldry and it was three days
old and the meat was too fat but I can't start
doing that now; and as for music I turned
to one of the B's, and as for Thought—and you know
what I mean by Thought—oh prune, oh apple
with the flesh exposed too long, I turned to the beaver
who, by his chewing, given the way he chews,
and by the sapling he abandoned there in
the low-lying bush above my water I knew
he had to leave and his thinking was interrupted,
although he changed my river and brought the birds
out in his wake, and with his wooden chips,
one of which I carry to prophesize,
he made a dry path for his murderers.

BATTLE OF THE BULGE

The way a fly who dies in sugar water,
he couldn't find a way to lift his wings
out of there, they were so heavy, the way
a plant doesn't need that rich a dirt, the way
it chokes from too much love, the way
I lay on the ground, I dug a hip hole, I slept
with grass, and dirt, the way Amos Hennesy
wore a red flannel shirt, and a tie, he was
Dorothy Day's friend—you know that saint?—it was
my own costume for years, he was in prison
with Berkman—in Atlanta—Berkman was there
for shooting and stabbing Frick, Hennesy for
conscience; I met Hennesy on Spruce Street
in 1958, the same year I met
Jack Lindeman who lost his hearing in Belgium,

the winter of 1944, he lives in
Fleetwood, P.A. and we communicate by
fax—I never heard him ask for pity
nor did we ever talk about that winter, he
introduced me to Dorothy Day and published
his poems in the *Catholic Worker*—and Marvin Hadburg,
he whom *I* pity, he was drafted when the
government was desperate and sent to
Fort Benning, Georgia for four weeks training
and then to Bastogne three days before Christmas
where he spent a week in a barn and came home
with both feet frozen a day or two short of two months
some of the flesh cut off, as I remember,
a gold discharge button in his lapel,
selling underwear again in his father's store,
his head very small, his shoulders hunched, his mouth
always open—I would say he was a
collector of feathers for the Achaean archer
Teucer of the incurved bow, whose shoulder
Hector smashed with a rock, just where the clavicle
leads over to the neck and breast, thus deadening
his wrist and fingers, I would say that Ajax
knocked him down when passing by and Zeus,
deflector of arrows and breaker of spears, the father
of slaughter without end, he pissed on him.

Among GERALD STERN'*s many honors are the Lamont Prize, the National Book Award, a Guggenheim fellowship, three* NEA *awards, a fellowship from the Academy of Arts & Letters, and the Ruth Lilly Prize. He taught at the* Writers' Workshop *at the University of Iowa until his retirement in 1995, and today lives in New Jersey and continues to write both poetry and prose. His latest books are* American Sonnets *(Norton 2002) and* What I Can't Bear Losing: Notes From a Life *(Norton 2003).*

Rachel Tzvia Back

On Methods of Concealment (a Manual)

1) Camouflaging Underground Caches:

Consider ratio of rocks to dirt to sand
Size of the stones how pale and
How marked with black ore veins

Count paces to each path and paved road
Within a mile circumference from
And all track locations with exact
Bearing whether in use or rusted
Under weeds

Do not dig where water may gather
Do not lay tools on the ground in
The dark do not return by day
Desire to see the disappearance

2) Burning of Evidence:

Only where fire can be controlled
Behind doors, away from winds
Ash and blackened half
Burnt paper slowly closing palms.

Ignite small amounts to allow
Rapid extinguishing if detected
Be aware that smoke lingers longest
On hair curtains clothes, in windowless
Quarters. Beware of staining

3) Covering Tracks:

Walk backwards as though before
Royalty or god facing own boot
Prints sweat droplets tracked-in
Dirt of other places to sweep

Away your trail with branches to
Leave only blurred leaf marks. Avoid
Wearing patterned soles. Avoid
Sand paths water patches.

Step lightly. Carry as little as you
Can *come back as you were* at the site
before the lowing before leaving
before

4) Destroying by Water:

To undo messages soak paper
Till fully steeped water will loosen
All holds then rub your finger over
Ink marks until meaning floats *before*

Storms tracked to gulf before nets
Not pulled in boats not called back
Ropes heavy in my hands in my arms
Other subversions come back as you

Were I cannot

Destroy remaining paper pulp keep
No notes *night*

Refusing its stars

5) Codes:

Or love if possible
Before giving back

Bone by light by bone

Bravo Lima Bravo
Signal   *signal*
If you are under

No undue pressure

RACHEL TZVIA BACK *was raised in Buffalo, New York and now lives in the Galilee. Her collections include* The Buffalo Poems *(Duration Press, 2003) and* Azimuth *(Sheep Meadow Press, 2001). She is also the author of* Led by Language, *a ground-breaking monograph on the work of American experimental poet Susan Howe. Back's translations of the selected poetry of Lea Goldberg are forthcoming in spring 2005 from Toby Press.*

Alan Shapiro

Three Poems

RED BUD LEAVES

After the downpour, in the early evening,
late sunlight glinting off the rain drops sliding
down the broad backs of the red bud leaves
beside the porch, beyond the railing, each leaf
bending and springing back and bending again
beneath the dripping,
             between existences,
ecstatic, the souls grow mischievous, they break rank,
swerve from the rigid Vs of their migration,
their iron destinies, down to the leaves
they flutter in among, rising and settling,
bodiless, but pretending to have bodies,

their weightlessness more weightless for the ruse,
their freedom freer, their as ifs nearly not,
until the night falls like an order and
they rise on one vast wing that darkens down
the endless flyways into other bodies.

Nothing will make you less afraid.

NEWS CONFERENCE

Invisible slow tumbling drift of ash
over the smoking city sifting flake
by flake down out of the lethe of itself
in a freedom of dispersal beyond belief—

What was the lesson? steam of whose rage?

particle of particle of dry
continuous blizzard of the long extinguished
fires of what, in the name of what, now fall
as new flakes falling among the not yet nameless—

What were the numbers saying when they spoke for themselves?

over the hot hoods of the jammed traffic,
the flipped up middle fingers of the late
for work, and horn blare, cry of sirens near
and far, but never farther never nearer

What shining city on what hill exactly?

over the weeping prophet's back as he bends
to kiss the footprints of the led away,
and into the footprints, too, when he rises, till
there are no footprints, and there is no prophet

What call? What visionary dream? What now?

only the gate trampled, the rampart broken,
the smoldering bus, and shoe; only the soon
forever noiseless drifting of the ashes
of the exhalation of the long exhaled.

IN THE AFTERMATH OF A NATIONAL CATASTROPHE

In the first days afterward,
and at night especially,
mostly at night, we noticed
how quiet the sky had grown.

Sky suddenly quieter
than all but the oldest among us
could ever remember, and yet
to all of us it felt

like something given back,
restored, something that
belonged less to ourselves
than to the species, and less

the species' than the planet's,
earth circled once again
by only a vapor trail
of stars and the spaces between them!

No one would say a word
about this. On and off
the air, in every one
of our exchanges, our civil

cries and formulations,
not one of us would say
how good it felt to look
up and not see, not hear

any sign of us at all.
Embarrassed, even ashamed
of our relief, nobody
could say how good it felt

to think that by the time
the light our planet casts
has reached the nearest stars
our moment will be over.

ALAN SHAPIRO's *last book,* Song and Dance, *was published by Hough-ton Mifflin in 2002; his new book,* Tantalus in Love, *will be published in 2005.*

Alicia Ostriker

Tearing the Poem Up
and Eating It

You shall not oppress a stranger; for you know the heart
of the stranger, for you were strangers in Egypt
—Exodus 23:9
—in memory of Yitzhak Rabin

I

Take this, they said
Handing it to me
As if I were a prophet or a wise woman
As if a poem were something healing
As if a poem nourished
Not only itself, the life of language
Which certainly is worth nothing
Next to a biological life—
What are you saying?
Do you think the life of an insect
Is worth more than the life of a poem?

In childhood I did—
That is exactly what I thought
An ant, a pink-grey worm on the wet sidewalk
Was worth everything

II

Dear God, they say your justice is like rain, they also call you
A compassionate God, therefore I wanted to believe
These rivers of prophecies sluicing your Mediterranean streets
With running images of seedtime and harvest, of swords beaten
Into ploughshares, the knowledge of the heart of the stranger
Because we were strangers in Egypt, I wanted to believe

Justice and compassion pour through the lifeblood of your poem,
Your book, which can never be killed, but tell it to the bloody
      plaza
Tell it to the stone of sacrifice
Where the sons finally rise to slay the father
Tell it to the assassin's rabbi and his grandmother
Speak the poem to her oranges and fish

III

I stroll the lively boulevard of middle eastern history,
I visit the marketplace of thieves, drunks and saints
Warriors, prostitutes, ruin, nothing is new,
Zeal like a tough many-legged insect
Pestiferous, running and biting, indestructible,
Juice and seeds liberated by a shooting,
Hope like a manhole the clown falls into,
Wind of the spirit flows toward the aperture
Like gnats pouring into throats of birds,
A man like a pink-gray worm on the sidewalk,
Compassion and justice like raped girls after a party,
Of whom one asks, What were they drinking,
Why did they dress in skirts so short?

—Tearing the poem up and eating it
Will get me nowhere. Better to burn than to marry
What demands to be married, what offers its ring

Of spurious safety on condition that I sell my birthright
Of hope and forget to remember the heart of the stranger
And better to write than to burn
And best to clear a path for the wind

IV

At the funeral one of the ministers produced
What will obviously be the icon of this martyrdom:
The sheet of paper bearing the words of the peace song
He sang at the rally ten minutes before his assassination.
The paper was folded into quarters and stained
With an irregular shape of blood from where
It was in his pocket, fire and blood

You wonder at funerals why nobody bursts out laughing.

His granddaughter touchingly said to the microphone that she
Knew angels would bear him to heaven and perhaps they will, who
Am I
To doubt

V

Responsa

The rabbi said to his son:
I will give you ten gold coins
If you can tell me where God is
The boy answered:
I will give you twenty
If you can tell me where he is not

The moral:
If blood still stains the paper
It is God's blood,

Maggid

Is it not?

VI

Yet those who believe you chose them
break the bones of the unchosen
Those who trust in your righteousness
study death's secret handshake
Those who remember you promised them the land
sow it with corpses
Those who await messiah
dream of apocalypse
in which their enemies burn—
I speak of all your countries, my dear God.

ALICIA OSTRIKER *has published ten volumes of poetry, most recently The Volcano Sequence, and has twice been a finalist for the National Book Award. Her poems appear in numerous anthologies of Jewish poetry. This poem will appear in her forthcoming book* No Heaven, *due spring 2005. She is also the author of The Nakedness of the Fathers: Biblical Visions and Revisions, a combination of midrash and autobiography. Ostriker is Professor of English at Rutgers University.*

Rachel Zucker

Graven Image Envy: A Statement of Jewish Poetics

There are two reasons I am not a painter. First, in order to become a painter I would have had to cross a steep cultural divide that valued words over image, story over form, sound over sight. Not only was there was nothing in my family—a clan of wordsmiths and story tellers—that would have led me to canvas and paintbrush, but my Jewish education devalued and feared the visual arts: making painting and sculpture comes dangerously close to making idols.

The second reason I am not a painter is that I have no talent for painting. But this is hardly relevant. After all, I had no talent when I began at thirteen years old to (too) earnestly dedicate myself to the task of writing. No, I locate the main obstacle in my thwarted career as a painter in the religious and later cultural prohibition against the rendering of graven images.

And I understand this uneasiness, for I see God in a well-proportioned golden calf.

A good painting makes my jaw drop, my skin itch—it gives off a luminescent allure like forbidden fruit or a bad boyfriend. I envy. I want. I envy the burnished Buddha. Can't help but adore the beatific Madonna and baby Jesus, weep for the pierced-through portraits of word-made-flesh. Even after art turned away from the "religious" I still see God. Idols. Graven images.

Rothko made portraits of human emotion so accurate that when I first saw them I felt a wave of sadness so powerful I had to sit down on the floor. In Pollack and Kandinsky I see a record of the human body, of movement, of desperate energy, anger, joy. Julia Margaret Cameron, Rembrandt, Chuck Close, Vermeer, Helen Frankenthaler, Agnes Martin. Idols. Images.

At home I face my desk away from windows, toward the blank wall. But for the past few months I've had this reproduction of Gerhard Richter's painting, "Betty," on my desk. In it Richter's daughter is positioned facing the viewer but "caught" looking away. It is a painstakingly rendered painting of a snapshot with the tactile immensity of hours and hours of brushwork and the exuberant spontaneity of its original photographic medium. Into this painting I read various narratives about Richter and German history, the history of painting, the history of photography, of the relationship between men and women, fathers and daughters. But, ultimately, what moves me, what makes me indescribably compelled and wounded each time I see the image is, of course, that I see myself in it.

I see myself in Richter's brush trying so willfully, desperately, to capture, to hold, to describe, to make life from clay and dust, to make "Betty" live even as she looks away, away from the frame toward some distraction—some "real life" event the canvas can't contain. I see myself in the daughter-subject, in the way my family looks at me—carefully, longingly, but always askance, askew, glancingly, mistakenly. The way the culture, history, even my own attempts at self-portraiture, autobiography, ultimately fail to look me full-in-the-face, to see me head-on.

I could not make the image. Like a good Jew, the daughter of gem-dealers who were the grandsons of Rabbis I found my path in the word. And like the great-granddaughter of Rabbis I've stretched the rules to the limit. I do not render images—the word made flesh, the flesh made God. But because of what I have always and *only* been interested in—describing the complexity of human experience even if I'm only describing the back of someone's head—I've settled down to make the flesh made word. Schooled, trained, constrained in the medium of language, I find I have a talent for it, a taste for it.

And so far none have taken me to task for making portraits of Greek goddesses, virgin Marys, young mothers uncannily like myself—portraits of the human, the supernal, raw despair, colossal hubris of the individual. So far no bolt of lightning has struck me down for trying to make poems that breathe like golems, haunt like dybbuks and shine like golden calves.

Four Poems

SEX

Wane, wax, wobble.
My mind is a map of hunger.

They say Abulafia could stop his heart
with one letter. *Alef*

lodged in his semi-lunar valve.

Small *e* after breath
is what I do to keep living.

CODARY

Once you were a type, kind, tide.
But became a singularity.

Maggid

I stopped breathing.

Where the husband's orbit overlaps: darkness.
No light can be shed on what lies beyond this

and to say it never happened or
nothing improper...

the gravitational sheer,
harsh polarity

of wanting.

RHYME, LASCIVIOUS MATCHMAKER

Each time I try to—
here comes my husband again and

my mind, I'm describing; context.

Forgive me, anemone, my green clearing.
You are no still pool, but actual.

If I showed you my skull below the skin
then threw out the skin would you wipe clean

the bone? A thin gold wire

prevents my jaw from metaphor or
pastoral wandering.

Your V-neck suggests—
The bruised way you sit—

What to do with your lips—

THE SECRET ROOM

Isn't hidden. Nor filled with goods
or bodies. This feeling—

strip the wallpaper,
knock for panels—

I can't explain it—is always,
I think your gaze made it.

I say what I don't intend
so as to say something of

this tending, tendency, tender
unsayable place I mean to take you.

RACHEL ZUCKER *is the author of two collections of poetry:* Eating in the Underworld *and* The Last Clear Narrative. *She lives in New York City with her husband and two sons.*

VI. Archives

Before she ever heard of the Statue of Liberty, before she took up the cause of the huddled masses and devoted herself to the plight of her fellow Jews, Emma Lazarus took up the theme of immigration in this melodrama of art and dissolution, of drugs, gambling, and illicit sex, and of the American Dream. —Eds.

Emma Lazarus

The Eleventh Hour

Sergius Azoff was a lucky fellow. It was little more than a year since he had landed, friendless and penniless, in New York, with a barbarous name utterly unfamiliar to American artists and critics; yet already he had taken his place as undisputed master in the instruction of his art, and as the most brilliantly gifted young painter in the town. His was the good fortune, not only to have his genius recognized by dilettanti and by his brother craftsmen, but to become, by a happy chance, the favorite of the blind goddess of fashion. Never before had so many of the wealthiest merchants' and bankers' daughters been inspired with a zealous devotion to Art; and, whatever stage of advancement their culture had attained, all seemed now to have but one ambition,—to become the pupils of Azoff either to enter upon their auspicious career under the direction of so efficient a guide, or to receive from him the finishing touches of style, the final ideas as to color and tone, the vigorous boldness of brush which he best knew how to impart.

At this hour of high noon, his studio is invariably filled with his fair young feminine disciples,—for young and fair without exception are the six or eight American ladies diligently at work around the artist's easel. From so-called New York "society," it were difficult to select any group of women under thirty years of age, of whom a majority do not possess graceful figures and pleasing faces. But Azoff's pupils are the fine flower of the best, and as the bright February sunshine streams down upon them from the high window-top, it illuminates an unbroken array of genuine American beauties. Here are the large, expressive eyes; the fair, delicate complexions, neither sallow nor too highly colored, but of an aristocratic paleness; the clean-cut profiles; the coquettish, laughing mouths; the abundant hair, ranging through every variety of shade, from the blue-black of yonder tall girl, in whose veins flows a mixture of Austro-Spanish blood and who holds herself with the haughty grace of a huntress-Diana, to the crisp golden curls of the blonde who bends her dainty head and short-sighted blue eyes close over her sketch.

But Azoff evidently does not regard his charming class with any eyes but those of an artist and a teacher. He moves from one to another with counsel, help, encouragement, or, most rarely, words of praise; to him the face of the most beautiful suggests nothing but the indolent, petulant nature, the flippant mind, and the bungling hand which accompany it. What he prizes incalculably beyond the attractions of his lady-pupils, is the severe art-conscience, the religious devotion to the ideal, which he finds in the poor crippled boy who steals an occasional evening hour to develop a divine gift, and whom Azoff counts as his only worthy disciple. His morning visitors, on the contrary, are simply cultivating an "elegant accomplishment;" they are neither desirous nor capable of producing anything of real value or beauty. Yet, no; this perhaps is overstating or understating the truth. One, at least, among them has, if not the innate talent, yet the sincere ambition of the artist. Whatever Ellen Bayard does, she does with her whole heart; and though her original gift is probably the most meager of her class, and her bright hazel eyes are the least accurate in their report of nature, yet Azoff finds in guiding and instructing her the nearest approach to sympathy and pleasure which his irksome hours of tuition afford.

Watch her as she sits utterly absorbed in her work. One would say that she was the youngest of the group, so slight and supple is her frame, so child-like and pure the expression of her face, and so youthful is the effect conveyed by the simple arrangement of her braided chestnut hair. Yet she is already a wife and a mother, to whom, in her social circle, her girlish name of Ellen perpetually clings with a sort of aroma of maidenhood, but who is only known to Azoff as Mrs. Richard Bayard.

Sergius Azoff himself is not the least picturesque figure in the studio, as he bends his tall, dark head over his pupils' work. He is apparently between twenty-five and thirty years of age, and he possesses that rarest and most desirable of physical gifts—a presence. He is one of the few men who seem to fill and animate with a majestic grace even a large, bare apartment, and whose stately carriage and harmonious proportions render them conspicuous in a crowded assemblage. He had the pose of head, the commanding stature, and the dignified elegance of movement which one looks for in a prince, but which one is more apt to find in a great actor. So marked was this combination of strength and virile beauty in his frame that, as in a fine statue, the face became of secondary importance. It was pale and swarthy, surrounded by a full, dark beard; the nose was thin and aquiline; from the broad white brow the short hair waved upward in crisp brown ripples, and the round, dark-gray eyes were unusually large and luminous. If any feature inclined to the expression of weakness, it was the full, somewhat sensuous mouth; but this was the least likely to be remarked, for in repose it was almost hidden behind the thick, silky mustache and heavy beard, and when animated by laughter or speech, the brilliant teeth alone attracted attention. A grave, melancholy air, however, habitually overclouded Azoff's face, and, as may be supposed, did not detract from the sympathy which his romantic personality inspired. Whether by nature, or because he happened to live now among strangers, he was the reverse of communicative in regard to himself and his belongings, and none of his American friends had any positive knowledge of his real inner life. Any one who had felt sufficiently interested, however, during the past six weeks, to observe him closely, could not have failed to notice that this overhanging veil of melancholy had almost daily perceptibly deepened and darkened, and his original expression of serious thought had been succeeded by one of harassed fatigue and despondency.

The slender stock of actual information which the town possessed in regard to Azoff's history was more than counterbalanced by the variety and extravagance of the versions supplied by the "pipe of rumor, blown by surmises, jealousies, conjectures." He was a noble Polish refugee; a Russian prince in disguise; a dangerous adventurer; he was the disinherited son of a high Russian dignitary, degraded from his native rank in his own aristocratic country by his artist proclivities and Bohemian associates; he was a Hungarian nobleman, whose stormy youth had already exhausted a magnificent fortune, and for whom the cultivation of his talent was not an end, but only a means of redeeming his debts. All these suppositions, however contradictory in details, agreed in general coloring and in two essential features,— that Mr. Azoff had noble blood in his veins and a bar sinister in his escutcheon. Those who knew him best, knew that he was neither a Pole, a Hungarian, nor a Russian, but born in Roumania, of mixed parentage; and, among all his friends, the Bayards alone knew, further than this, that his father was dead, and his mother, a Russian lady, still lived in St. Petersburg with her widowed daughter.

The clock strikes the half-hour, and there is a general rustle of gowns and movement of departure among the students. Portfolios are taken out, sketches laid aside, and hats, jackets, and gloves are donned for the street. All the ladies, in bidding good-morning, exchange a few gracious, unprofessional words with Mr. Azoff, whom they condescend to treat as an equal and a friend. Mrs. Bayard, however, who slowly arranges her hat and furs, and is the last to leave, has a quite peculiar note of cordial kindness in her vibrant, sympathetic voice as she lingers to speak with her master. That just perceptible tone of condescension, which Azoff feels rather than hears in the voices of his other pupils, is altogether missing in hers. She treats him, not as her equal, but her superior.

"I could not go away to-day, Mr. Azoff, without asking if you had better news from St. Petersburg yet?"

"You are very kind to remember my troubles," answered he, gravely. "I heard only yesterday that my mother is out of danger. She writes herself a few lines in my sister's letter to tell me that she is convalescent."

"I am so very glad," said Mrs. Bayard, in her simple, earnest way. "Then you are quite free from all anxiety?"

"I am quite free from all anxiety," he replied, with a deep sigh, not of relief, but of heavy oppression. Mrs. Bayard looked at him wonderingly, as if seeking the key to the contradiction between his words and his manner. He seemed discomfited by her kindly glance, and went on hurriedly, "I am doubly glad that I shall not be obliged to go home again. If the news had not been better by this mail, I should certainly have left New York, where I am just beginning to feel that I have friends."

"It is something to hear you say that, at least," replied Mrs. Bayard, smiling. "I began to believe you did not value the friendship of Americans."

He started, his pale face flushed, and his eyes beamed with a singular emotion. With an impulsive movement, he took both her hands in his own.

"Dear Mrs. Bayard, if that be a reproach, forgive me! Believe me, I am neither indifferent nor ungrateful to the generous kindness I have received from your warmhearted Americans, and, above all, from yourself. Forgive me if I seem unappreciative; I have been very much harassed."

"I did not intend it as a reproach," said Mrs. Bayard, quietly withdrawing her gloved hands and taking up her muff; "I must altogether disclaim your gratitude before it is due, but I should like to feel that your American friends will some day deserve it. *Apropos*, or rather, *mal apropos*, Mr. Bayard has been buying some pictures lately. He has picked up, as he thinks, a genuine Titian, besides some modem trifles. He told me to ask if you would care to come see them. Will you dine with us informally to-day?"

"With all the pleasure in the world."

"Till seven o'clock, then," said Mrs. Bayard, moving toward the door.

"Are you walking, or may I have the honor of seeing you to your carriage?" asked Mr. Azoff.

"Thanks,—no. I should prefer not. I know my way through these corridors now," she replied, with a charming smile.

Mrs. Bayard, with all her simplicity, rarely lost sight of conventionalities, and did not care to be singled out among Mr. Azoff's pupils for his too frequent attentions, in this crowded art building where every studio had eyes and tongues. He opened the door and held it wide, saluting her with that haughty yet deferential grace peculiar to Sclavonic races, and developed by their characteristic dances. She passed out, leaving behind her a sort of wave of warm violet perfume, glided down the dusty staircase, and stepped into the coach that stood awaiting her, while an expression of puzzled thought came over her child-like face as she leaned back on the cushions and was rolled away.

A few moments later, Sergius Azoff locked his studio door behind him, and went out to deliver his weekly lecture to the pupils of the "Turner Institute," and then, again lessons, lessons and lessons, till within half an hour of the time when he had promised to present himself at Mrs. Bayard's.

II.

Mrs. Bayard was an arch-woman, simple and cunning, vain and disinterested, noble and petty, capable of entering with ardent enthusiasm into the thoughts and feelings of others, yet always retaining in the fervor of her generous emotion an undefined pleasant consciousness of her own sympathetic qualities. She resembled ten thousand other women already ten thousand times described, and yet fundamentally indescribable. A little more agreeable, perhaps, a little gentler, fairer to see, and more naive than many of her sisterhood, but intrinsically the same creature of undisciplined imagination, of impossible logic and magnetic intuition.

To-day, from the moment she left the studio till now, when she presides at her little circular dinner-table, around which are seated her husband and Mr. Azoff, she has not been able to forget the latter's singular agitation after the drawing-lesson; she could have sworn that his eyes had grown moist and his colorless face had flushed. She fancies she can discern in the artist's whole manner and attitude in her presence the germ of that which, if he be a man of honor, he must stifle in embryo to prevent its development into a bitter, poisonous fruit. And yet she, one of the gentlest and sweetest of her sex, who would not willingly crush the life out of an insect, and who entertains a genuine sympathy and friendship for the isolated, gifted young stranger, has, nevertheless, felt all through the day a complacent sort of pleasure, a subdued, triumphant sense of power, in imagining his unhappiness. She has not put her thought into words even in her own mind; it has all floated vaguely, yet persistently, within her idle little brain, and has not in the least diminished—nay, it has even added zest to—her interest in the performance of her household duties and to the affectionate greeting with which she met her husband upon his return home. Poor Mr. Azoff! he is so alone, so unlike the people around him, and consequently so susceptible to kindness, so sensitive to all impressions. And she is so securely sheltered in her happy haven, so safe under the protecting shield of her love for Dick, from even the threat of danger. None the less has she selected this evening her most coquettish gown, whose soft, clinging folds of sky-blue crape and Elizabethan ruff and trimmings of broad, yellowish lace, admirably set off the whiteness of her throat and the fresh, delicate tint, as of early spring flowers, of her round, wistful face, with its fawn-like eyes and glossy dark hair.

Mr. Bayard was a rather slight young man of medium size, but his well-knit figure gave the impression of elastic, sinewy strength. The intense blackness of his straight, Indian-like hair (whose stray locks were perpetually falling over his forehead) and of his thick, bold, perfectly horizontal eyebrows, heightened the pallor of a skin as fair as an infant's. His smooth-shaven face, bare of mustache or beard, gave him at a little distance the air of a school-boy, though he had already passed his thirtieth year, but a nearer examination revealed certain inexorable lines about the brow and mouth which can only be stamped by years of mature thought. It is rare to see such eyes as Dick Bayard possessed. They were neither those of an Apollo nor of a man of genius, but they were emphatically those of an honest man,—so limpid, so keen, and so fearless, they looked out from under the frank, square brow as if they had nothing to conceal, and as if nothing could be concealed from them. Decidedly he was not a handsome man, but his expression was one of winning loyalty and sincerity, and the weird, almost uncanny effect produced by his pale skin and elfin hair, together with a certain gnome-like uncouthness about his presence, irresistibly attracted the glance again and again. He had but little acquaintance with that infinitesimal division of our globe which arrogates to itself the title of "the world," and his natural timidity, already a morbid one, was increased by the consciousness of his inexperience. He was consequently seldom understood by the people he met, more especially when these happened to be Europeans. An intelligent American is apt to feel a peculiar interest in any deviation from the high road of convention, and there was something about Dick Bayard which continually piqued the curiosity, and thus appealed to one of the strongest instincts of his compatriots. But to the cultivated, polished foreigners whom Mrs. Bayard's exquisite grace attracted to the house, the young man's sylvan, untamed naturalness (we know of no other term for it) seemed only the boorishness of the uncivilized American, and his odd, abrupt ways led them to the general belief; which they did not hesitate to express, that he was *"un peu toqué."*

Azoff, however, was not among the holders of such an opinion. He had not waited till to-day (when Dick, in a discussion on art, had given evidence of critical judgment, broad culture and acute insight) to know that Mr. Bayard was a man of real significance. He had begun by covertly studying the young American as a faun, a kobold, a subject for a fantastic sketch of moonshine madness, the leader of a dance of gnomes. How effectively the light of torches could be made to bring out the contrast between his eerie white face and wild, black, floating locks! What a weird grace his features would acquire if surrounded by the proper accessories of haunted forest and fallow marsh-land! But every day of nearer acquaintance led Azoff farther from this first superficial view, and deepened his astonished admiration and respect for the young man's intellectual and moral force. This change, however, may have been partly owing to other causes than that of a more intimate acquaintance; for, as the artist's despondency and dissatisfaction with himself and his own work daily increased, he may have been disposed to think less of the mere aesthetic and picturesque, and attach a higher value to straightforward, indomitable integrity.

"Richard, I am almost inclined to quarrel with Mr. Azoff," said Mrs. Bayard, "over his severity to me. Do you know what he obliged me to do with the pretty little river-sketch I showed you, and that I was so proud of having made? I had to rub out every line, and begin it all over again. He was gracious enough to say that the composition was tolerable, but then, the drawing! And yet, I looked over Nina Morton's landscape and saw faults just as glaring as my own, and he allowed her to carry it home in triumph!"

"Perhaps that is because Mr. Azoff feels that you are capable of better things, Ellen, and that Miss Nina Morton is not," said Mr. Bayard, turning with an inquiring glance from his wife to Azoff.

"I should not have dared put it in just those words," replied Azoff, smiling; "but that is the true explanation. If Mrs. Bayard knew of my exacting rigor in regard to my own work, she would feel that my severity is the highest compliment I can pay a pupil. To prove this, I will make you a humiliating confession. I wiped out of existence, yesterday, Mr. Bayard, the sixth attempt at a beginning of the picture you were good enough to order from me three months ago."

"What a shameful pity!" cried Mrs. Bayard. "How can you be so cruel to yourself? Dick, I saw this 'attempt,' as Mr. Azoff calls it, and it promised to be a perfect gem. It was a Russian interior, but genuinely Russian,—it looked like a leaf out of Tourguéneff,—and painted in a style of which we have seen no specimens yet in this country. Why did you destroy it, Mr. Azoff?"

"It is scarcely a case in point, after all," replied Azoff, thoughtfully. "I destroyed it for precisely the opposite reason from that which made me ask you to work over yours, because I have lost faith in myself."

He spoke so seriously that Mrs. Bayard felt a conventional compliment would be out of place. She looked at him in surprise, and was silent.

Richard fastened his penetrating eyes on the artist and asked in his direct way:

"Do you think it is your occupations here and the commercial American atmosphere that have materialized your life and undermined your confidence in yourself?"

Sergius Azoff raised his eyes to Mr. Bayard, but they quailed before that candid, searching glance; his heart glowed with a grateful warmth, for he felt that he had spoken and had been understood, but he shrank at the same time from so close a scrutiny, as if Mr. Bayard's eyes had really the power to see behind the veil.

"I cannot tell," he replied, slowly, after a short pause, "if the fault be in myself or in my circumstances. I feel as if my brain were being gradually ground into a dry powder by this tread-mill routine. A man whose eyes, and nerves, and patience have been continuously overstrained six days out of seven is scarcely able to bring a fresh set of organs to bear upon an original production on the seventh. My ideal has certainly not risen any higher since my arrival here, and yet my work gives me less and less satisfaction. Ten years of this life might make me financially independent;—they would certainly be my ruin as an artist."

Dick Bayard had a curious way, when deeply interested, of losing himself in his own thoughts and allowing them to leap over such broad generalizations that when he spoke again his words seemed wide of the original mark. The oracular, half-intelligible phrases which he uttered on such occasions had strengthened the prevailing belief that he was a trifle unsound; but upon any one who had faith in him these very speeches made a profound impression, and if such a one would try to follow out the course of reasoning which must necessarily have preceded them, he would often find a positively startling, almost demonic intuition at their root. So it was in this case. Mr. Bayard's head was almost buried in his breast, his eyes had a singular, dreamy look, and he spoke, with the voice of a man only half awake, not *to* but *at* Azoff.

"He has not properly assimilated himself yet. America is not a bad *milieu* for the true artist. And then, half truths are no truths. We know his secret."

Azoff was like a wounded man who feels the surgeon's probe reach the very bottom of his hurt. What did this strange American know of his, Sergius Azoff's, life-secrets, that he should speak of them with the voice of a prophet!

But Mrs. Bayard interposed:

"Why, Dick, what are you muttering about?"

"Oh, I was thinking, Ellen dear," replied Dick, with a start, passing his hand over his forehead, tossing back his hair, and smiling like a sphinx at his guest. "Tell us, Mr. Azoff, how you happened to come to America."

"There is scarcely anything to tell," said Azoff; "it was partly accident. In the east of Europe, where the nineteenth century ideas are fermenting no less actively than in the west, yet where the spirit of feudalism is still the breath and soul of social institutions, you can have no conception of the imaginary glories with which we invest America. When I was a boy of fourteen at the Gymnasium, I knew by heart the Declaration of Independence, and I designed, with a set of lads as enthusiastic as myself, a little socialistic community, based upon American principles, with which we were later to overturn thrones, principalities, and powers. That, of course, was broken up before I left the Academy, but the enthusiasm itself did not die out. In Bucharest, in Petersburg, in Paris, my dream of America, my ardor for republican ideas grew with my growth, and everywhere I found ambitious youth,—Roumanians, Bulgarians, Frenchmen, Russians, Bohemians from all parts of the world,—artists, students, poets,—whoever had felt the cramping influence of ignorant legislation, whoever had conceived freedom, or desired progress, or loved beauty,—to stimulate me and participate in my illusion. Perhaps the peculiar circumstances of my life have made me suffer more from Old World prejudices, and have given me a more bitter aversion to the vicious distinctions of rank and caste, than my more fortunate college companions. At any rate, I am the only one who has had the courage or energy to endeavor to realize our common dream. Who knows? Perhaps—"

Azoff stopped abruptly.

"Perhaps they were wiser than you," said Mr. Bayard, finishing his phrase. "With them the illusion will slowly die a natural death under the ordinary influences of time and change, while you have crushed it at a blow by coming to see with your own eyes the practical working of the principles you cherished so long. Confess that that was what you wanted to say."

"I have found so many kind and noble hearts among the Americans," replied Azoff evasively, "that I feel like an ingrate if I attempt to express the peculiar disappointment I have experienced."

"But you cannot keep it a secret from your friends," said Mrs. Bayard. "Mr. Bayard and I have no intention of quarreling with you for the honor of our political institutions, but if you do not wish us to know that you sought something in America which you have not found, you must not speak so eloquently about the anticipation and let your face fall and your voice fade away so significantly when you talk of the reality."

"If you were to leave us now," said Richard, "no doubt you would paint a dismal picture to your old comrades of the modem Utopia. But patience, I say, patience, Mr. Azoff! Wait five years, three years, one year longer, till you have adapted yourself to the groove, and see if you cannot carry home a representation of the country and the people that shall correspond better with your youthful dreams."

"I cannot imagine myself fitting into any groove," said Azoff with a smile. "But you know I have not the habit of talking about myself;" he went on, "and indeed, since I have been in America, I have seemed to be surrounded by a wall of ice. Why is it that when I am with you, dear friends, the ice seems to melt? I experience an irresistible desire to talk of my life, my disappointments, my ambitions, even my *ennuis*. Bah!" he exclaimed, with a laugh and an entire change of tone; "it is because you are too good to me, and I abuse your goodness by becoming *ennuyeux* to you as well as to myself."

Dick was not pleased with Azoff's suddenly assumed carelessness, but Mrs. Bayard felt that the ice having been broken, nothing would be easier, if only it were not insisted upon at the moment, than to draw the artist back to the theme on which her curiosity had been so strongly excited. She answered therefore with a re-assuring smile:

"*Ennui* is a thing that neither Mr. Bayard nor I believes in, Mr. Azoff. Nothing can be *ennuyeux* as long as one is young and well and sane. Shall we go in now and see the Titian? Our coffee can be brought to us in the library." She rose and the two young men followed her into the adjoining room.

It was a gorgeous, warm, golden-toned picture, representing the full-length dazzling figure of the sleeping Venus voluptuously reclining beneath a wide-open window, beyond which spread a sunset sky illuminated by dusky golden clouds overhanging a somber landscape. Mr. Azoff in his enraptured admiration was as excited as a child; while Richard, with his solemn American air stood by with no other demonstration of pleasure than a gnome-like half-smile on his face. Mrs. Bayard watched them both for a little while, looking on in silence or responding sympathetically to the artist's delight, and then excusing herself to make sure that her baby was sleeping, she left her husband and Azoff alone. When she returned to the room a half-hour later, she found them quietly seated some distance from the Titian, and her quick eye noted that Mr. Azoff's face had become as calm and solemn as Richard's. He brightened up as she took her seat near them, however, and the ready tact and grace with which she entered into the conversation soon gave it a lively animation and flow.

For all three it was a memorable evening. Within Dick Bayard's heart a disinterested friendship was then first awakened toward this brilliant young stranger endowed with such remarkable physical and intellectual gifts, and yet whom he, the plodding American, instinctively desired to guard and protect as he might a weaker younger brother. Certain suspicions were aroused in his breast almost amounting to pangs of fear and misgiving. His peculiar mind dealt frequently with symbols and tropes, and his thoughts had a habit of painting themselves in pictures; to-night he could not exorcise the haunting vision of a flawless, superb vessel without a compass, dangerously drifting on a dark open sea.

Never before had Mrs. Bayard been so interested and charmed by the young foreigner who was at the same time her master and her protégé. He talked with the fire of genius on every subject that was broached, and his manner to her was so grateful, so earnest, so devoted, that her excitable mind and nerves were wrought to a pitch of almost painful exaltation. Then, too, she succeeded at last in gratifying, on at least one item, her feminine curiosity. Azoff chanced, in the most natural way, to divulge a romantic fact concerning his mother, of whom he had only spoken hitherto in vague terms of affection. They were talking of music, and Mrs. Bayard went to the piano to exemplify her idea of a certain song of Schumann's. When she rose, Azoff to her surprise, took the seat, and, respectfully differing from her conception, struck a few chords to illustrate his own.

"That is far better than my idea of the theme," she said. "But I never knew you were a musician."

"Nor am I," he replied, rising from the piano. "But it is only a chance that I am not. A taste for music was the first aptitude that developed itself in me, and I was destined to be an artist. It is a legitimate inheritance—my mother was a musician."

"An artist?" asked Mrs. Bayard.

"Yes, a pupil of Liszt, in the days when Liszt still gave lessons to his pupils. Her name was ———." And Azoff mentioned the name of one of the most widely renowned pianists of twenty-five years ago.

Mrs. Bayard knew how to express exactly the requisite amount of surprise and friendly curiosity, in order not to startle the habitually reserved stranger out of his unwonted confidential mood, and to draw from him a hundred interesting details of his mother's life and artistic career before she had adopted her present retired existence. It was easy to see that for this enthusiastic son the very air was sanctified which his mother breathed.

But most of all by Sergius Azoff was this evening never to be forgotten. The recollections of his home thus vividly awakened; the thrill of enjoyment aroused in him by the sight of such a work of art as his eyes had not rested upon since he left Europe; the whole atmosphere of luxury, of rest, and of sympathy which surrounded him in the Bayards' house, together with a myriad vague, beautiful dreams and ambitions mingling confusedly in his brain, caused his sensitive temperament a singular, powerful emotion. When he pressed his friends' hands at parting, and went out into the mild, spring-like

February midnight, he looked up at the familiar stars and felt that he was no longer an exile.

III.

A month had elapsed since Sergius Azoff had gone to see the Titian, and his visits to the Bayards had rapidly increased in frequency and length, and yet a quiet, trustful friendship was not established. He appeared more than ever subject to fits of depression, which he was either no longer able or no longer desirous to conceal, and, since the evening when he had talked so frankly about his feelings and his home, he had more than ever avoided all confidences concerning either himself or his family. He saw Mrs. Bayard often alone, and she would have been more or less than woman could she have failed to notice that her influence exercised a powerful sway over him. However moody, weary, or caustic he might feel, he was always tranquilized or cheered by her presence. He could not himself have told what it was that he found so exquisitely suave in her voice and manner,—why the delicate refinement of her slim white hands made such a pleasing impression upon him. As for Dick, Azoff grew less and less at ease in his presence. At times, he actually shunned that searching, loyal glance,—then again he would evince a feverish, almost childish desire to be with Dick, to win his friendship, to court and please him. But Dick was not a man to be courted. There was a great deal about Azoff which he neither liked nor approved, and, notwithstanding an underlying sentiment of mingled friendliness, admiration, and compassion, he did not hesitate to manifest his disapprobation in a repellent coldness and a reserve still greater than Azoff's own. For Azoff, however uncommunicative in regard to his personal affairs, being a man of the world and a man of talent, was generally a brilliant, animated talker; but Bayard, a thinker and a man of firm will, was silent to moroseness when those around him did not inspire his confidence or affection.

"Dick," said Mrs. Bayard to her husband one day after her return from the studio, "I am so sorry for Mr. Azoff. I am sure he must have some great trouble. He is simply ruining himself. He is gradually losing all his pupils. I told you the other day about two of the girls leaving him, and to-day three more of the class whose quarterly term was over, said they would not return."

"The man is throwing himself away," replied Dick between his teeth, "but that is no affair of mine."

"It is hard enough to see a man of his talent throwing himself away," said Mrs. Bayard, without heeding her husband's last phrase. "But it is not his fault that he is losing his pupils. He works as conscientiously with them as ever, but you know what New York fashion is. Nina Morton left him in a pet, and whatever example Nina Morton sets, half a dozen toad-eaters will follow. They will probably all go over to Mr. Brillonin, who is giving Mary Hunt lessons, and who will be the next favorite."

"It might not be the worst thing for Azoff if they did," answered Mr. Bayard. "To be 'the fashion' in New York is not the most desirable fate for a man with real grit in him. These mincing young ladies, with their feminine compliments and *frou-frou* of silk gowns around his studio all day, are enough to polish all the manhood off him. I don't know but that it would be advisable for you, too, Ellen, to drop him,—for his ultimate good, you know," and Mr. Bayard looked at his wife with his customary enigmatical smile.

"Richard, how queer you are!" cried she, half vexed. "If I didn't know you better, I should think you were as savage as the Indian you look like just now. Why are you so hard upon Mr. Azoff? If we all give him up he will starve."

"Perhaps, even that might be better than the life he is leading now," muttered Dick.

Mrs. Bayard's wide eyes opened wider.

"What do you know of his life, Dick? Isn't he a gentleman?"

"What do I know?" said Richard, thoughtfully; "I know nothing. But I don't trust him,—there is something wrong, and wicked, and weak in him. And why does he force himself upon me? I am tired of seeing him around, tired of hearing his name; we are not related to each other in the most remote degree. He is utterly uninteresting; let us say no more about him, Ellen."

And Ellen said no more about him. She had never seen her husband jealous, and a not altogether easy conscience whispered to her that perhaps this suspicious petulance and unusual deafness to an appeal to his charity, resulted from her own overwarm partisanship of the young man's cause.

That evening, Azoff was again at the Bayards', but he was not the only visitor. Ellen shuddered as she saw him enter the room. She had been ill at ease ever since her conversation with her husband; she was frightened at the possible consequences of her own rash vanity. Sergius Azoff was not to be trifled with, and she saw him with new eyes this evening; powerful of frame, with those fine, severe features, that transparent swarthy skin, and those fiery Eastern eyes—how could she ever have dreamed that it would not be playing a dangerous game to arouse the passions of such a man? To-night he was so pale as to look positively ill, and her anxious scrutiny revealed to her the full extent of the change that had taken place in his appearance during the past month; his face was thin and sunken, making conspicuous the high Wallachian cheekbones, and the strained, dissipated expression of the eyes seemed underscored as it were, by deep, almost violet-colored lines. It required an effort to receive him naturally, but he, on his part, appeared in a far more cheerful mood than usual. With a liveliness suggestive at moments of undue excitement, he talked to Mrs. Bayard and her guests; brilliant, witty, and eloquent, he left on the latter the impression of dazzling genius.

What Ellen Bayard had not dreaded least that evening, was the unfriendly attitude Richard would in all probability assume toward Azoff and the latter's possible resentment of it in his present singular excitement and unnatural tension of nerve. She had not guessed her husband amiss; his manner to the artist was cold, sullen, almost gruff. But she had been mistaken in regard to Mr. Azoff. So far from being irritated by this *brusquerie*, he evinced a more than ordinary deference to every word and movement of his host, and late in the evening, when he found himself for a moment separated from the others and alone with Mrs. Bayard, he whispered to her impulsively:

"Mrs. Bayard, your husband is my guardian angel."

She raised her face suddenly and inquiringly to his.

"Trust him and he will help you," she said quickly, and returned to her guests.

"Trust him and he will help you." The words rang in Sergius Azoff's ears; they haunted his brain for days, together with the gentle earnest glance that had accompanied them. And yet he lacked the moral courage to intrust to Richard Bayard, of all men, that which was preying upon his life. There was something so clean, so lofty, so chaste as it were, about the young American, that Sergius Azoff felt as if it would be almost like laying bare his soul to a woman, to confess himself to Dick. And then, if Dick had not been rich! But would it not be beggarly in him to reveal to this fortunate young man the humiliating straits to which his own evil luck and evil habits had reduced him?

But, if he would not confide in Richard, yet twice did accident reveal somewhat of that which he had fain so carefully suppressed. One night toward the middle of April, the Bayards' baby had fallen ill, and Dick, in consideration of his wife's anxiety, rather than lose time by calling one of the men-servants from the stable, had gone himself at two o'clock in the morning to summon the physician. He had but a few squares to walk, the streets were silent and deserted, and until he reached within a door or two of the doctor's dwelling, he met no living creature. It was doubtless the previous solitude which made more conspicuous the first human figure he encountered now. A tall, powerful man was approaching; at a distance of several feet he recognized Sergius Azoff. The two men stood face to face under a flaring street-lamp. Mr. Azoff was haggard and white; he was walking in a dogged, aimless way, with both hands in the pockets of a shabby, light-gray overcoat; his eyes were heavy and half closed, and he had the air of a somnambulist. He looked Richard full in the face without a gleam of recognition, and passed on. They were so close that his unfastened, flying overcoat brushed against Bayard, who was conscious at the same moment of a faint, sultry, peculiar odor. He looked back after Sergius Azoff, and saw that he staggered as he walked. A mingled expression of pain and astonishment crossed his features,—"The man is an opium-eater," he muttered, half articulately, and with bent head he hastened on his errand.

Richard never told his wife of this meeting with Azoff, but in his own mind he resolved to have all friendly, unprofessional intercourse between Ellen and the artist gradually cease. But he had no opportunity to take any active measures to this effect, for Azoff did not again appear at the house, and Mrs. Bayard, who still went regularly to the studio for her lessons, said that his whole manner toward her had changed and had become that of a social inferior, humble, respectful, almost deprecatory. He no longer spoke of anything but the work in hand, he seemed to feel that he had something to atone for, and only a remnant of his former pride appeared to prevent him from begging her forgiveness. Her quick eye noticed in glancing around the studio the gradual disappearance and finally the total absence of all the little superfluities and knickknacks which had formerly adorned it; it grew shabby, bare and poor. Knowing the haughty sensitiveness of the artist's temperament, she was firmly convinced that his rapidly increasing poverty was the sole barrier which had arisen between them. When she looked into his altered face, and observed the listless, tired movements of his stately frame, her whole heart seemed to melt in sympathy, and she longed to say something that would break through this unnatural formality, and make him give utterance to the trouble that oppressed him. Yet, day after day passed by, and she dared not say a word; she grew almost afraid of those strange, large, hungry eyes, that stern, set, impassive face. And what was the use of offering her sympathy and prevailing upon him to speak, when she was powerless unaided to help him? For she felt that Richard was no longer her ally; during the past two or three weeks, he had discouraged all allusion to Mr. Azoff; never before had Ellen known him so uncharitable and ungenerous. She saw clearly that very little would be required to make him forbid her continuing her lessons at the studio. There was no need, however, for his interference in this case. One morning Mrs. Bayard received a card from Mr. Azoff begging her to excuse him from that day's lesson, as he was obliged to be from home at the appointed hour. She said nothing of it to her husband, but the next time she went to the studio Mr. Azoff was not in. She returned home provoked, not only at the artist, but at herself, for the awkward position in which she was placed toward her husband, to whom she would now be forced to confess her former concealment, as well as her present annoyance. When she reached the house, however, she found a brief note awaiting her from Mr. Azoff in which he thanked her for her great kindness to him and begged permission to discontinue the lessons altogether for the present, as he was about to leave town. She was perplexed, pained, disappointed; the man was evidently determined to ruin himself; since he repelled his last friend. She showed the note to Richard, who read it in silence, and Azoff's name was not again mentioned between them.

The spring of 1877 was a beautiful season in New York. After a warm, rainy April succeeded a few days of midsummer heat, which brought out, as if by magic, the foliage and flowers in the streets, the gardens and the parks. A day or two of cooling showers restored the natural temperature, and in the beginning of May came that exhilarating brilliant weather when every hour even in the heart of the city, made sweet with the chirp of birds and the fragrance of flowers, seems a renewal of some covenant of joy. With Richard Bayard the enjoyment of Nature was a passion; he seemed nearer than most men to her heart; he knew the secrets of her weeds and herbs; he loved almost equally her heats and colds, her days and nights, her sunshine and storms. During the spring and early summer, he was in the habit of rising at five or six o clock, to walk for an hour or two in Central Park before the business of the day began. It was there on a bright Saturday morning, in the latter part of May, that occurred his second unexpected encounter with Sergius Azoff, still more singular than the last.

He had been walking some time, and was in haste to leave the Park, when he found himself at its extreme end, near the western boundary. If his time allowed, he would gladly continue to walk homeward, but he feared he should be obliged to cross the road at once and take the nearest streetcar that would carry him down town. He drew his watch from his pocket and found that it had stopped at six o'clock. He looked around for some one of whom he could inquire the precise hour. There was not even a policeman in sight, but a few yards away, on a lower grade, some workmen were repairing the road.

"My friend," he called down to one of them from a little distance, "can you give me the hour?"

The overseer consulted his goodly sized chronometer and informed Mr. Bayard that it was "exactly eight o'clock, barring five minutes."

By the side of the overseer, with his back to Richard, stood a tall, muscular man, pounding the stones with a paving-beetle. Under the shadow of his broad-brimmed straw hat, Richard could discern against the clear blue of the morning sky, a familiar, bearded half-profile.

"Good God!" he exclaimed, "it is Sergius Azoff."

But the laborer had averted his head, and the brawny back, in its coarse flannel shirt, no longer suggested the elegant figure of the artist. Mr. Bayard rubbed his eyes like a man awaking from a dream. He walked thoughtfully across the road, hailed the first car that passed, and within an hour was in his office.

IV.

There was no light burning in Mr. Azoff's studio, though night had long since fallen. Behind the high screen which divided that part of the room where the artist slept from the studio proper, was a tall window opening on a series of leads and roofs. Through the uncurtained glass the bright rays of the moon rendered visible a low iron cot, upon which slumbered heavily a man dressed in the red shirt and soiled, worn trowsers of a laborer. Sergius Azoff, overcome by the unwonted physical fatigue of a day of manual toil, had thrown himself upon his bed as he entered the studio, and had not stirred from the position in which he had fallen. That was three hours ago; it was now ten o'clock. Suddenly he awoke,—not partially and gradually, but thoroughly, all at once. His sleep had been so deep that he felt as if it had lasted all night. The clear radiance of the moon on the white coverlet seemed to startle him, and he rose hastily to a sitting posture and looked about him with the air of a man who has overslept the hour of an important event. No, it was not too late; another day had not yet dawned. He stretched himself wearily and went to the dressing-table, dipping his face and hands again and again in the cold, fresh water, until he felt all the heaviness and fumes of sleep washed from him; then he struck a light, sat down by a very disordered secretary, and began to write. His hands burned as if blistered; they felt hard, sore, benumbed; but that was of no consequence, his letter would not be very long. He wrote it as fast as his pen could move, and it ran as follows:

MY DEAR MR. BAYARD: I do not feel as if I need explain in any wise to you why I should burden you rather than another with the responsibility of fulfilling the last wishes of an unhappy man. In this hour, when every word represents to me its full significance, I wish to tell you that ever since I have known you, you have unconsciously exercised a powerful influence upon my actions; your chance words have often struck the very core of my malady; your severe silence and keen glance have made me pause and resist the proffered temptation. I cherished a superstitious feeling that from you, in some mysterious way, help was sure to come to me. I had never been a believer in Spiritualism, in supernatural agencies, in presentiments, in elective affinities, in any of the fantastic delusions with which wretched men have built up for themselves the dream of an independent soul-life. And yet to you, a man of such different habit, complexion, and race from myself, I felt at first sight drawn as to a brother. At one moment during the course of our acquaintance, I half fancied that I also, on my part, had inspired you with a certain degree of friendship, of sympathy—who knows?—of confidence, perhaps. But the moment passed, and I saw clearly that you turned from me with aversion and mistrust. The folly of my strange delusion has been conclusively proved by the result. I have been in grievous straits and you have not divined my necessity; I have despaired, and you have not heard my cry. But you need have been more than human were it otherwise, for my lips have remained sealed. You have been neither supernatural nor demonic, but my faith in you as a man of immaculate probity and adamantine will still subsists; myself I feel unstable as water, and therefore it is a natural polarity that attracts me to you.

I die by my own hand. I take my life with an absolutely clear and deliberate mind. In this act I cannot see any sin or any injury to a single human being, though I have carefully weighed every conceivable argument. I am tired of the burden, and I lay it aside. My earnest request to you is that as far as lies in your power you will use every means to prevent the fact of my suicide from reaching the ears of my mother. I inclose her address in Petersburg. You are the only man in America who knows her true name, and I beg of you, as an act of charity, to impart to her the news of my death as having occurred in a natural manner, and to tell her that my last thought, my last prayer was for her.

One more word: When I met you on the night of the 16th of April, in Waverley place, I was intoxicated with opium. Was it your glance that sobered me? I do not know; I had no control over myself at the time. I passed on, and knew that you despised me. I felt you look back at me,—your eyes seemed to burn into my flesh. I staggered and nearly fell. Since that night I have not tasted opium.

To Mrs. Bayard I send thanks, and thanks, and thanks. The voice, the pitying glance, the gentle presence of such women, are the only compensations with which Fate lightens the miseries of men.

I desire that the few artistic effects left in my studio shall go to Joseph Bradford, the crippled boy, to whom I have given lessons since my arrival in America.

SERGIUS AZOFF

As he finished in a firm, though rapid, hand the signing of his name, he drew a deep breath, threw aside the pen and raised his eyes. Richard Bayard stood before him.

His arms were crossed over his breast, his head downcast, his eyes intently fixed upon Sergius Azoff; his straight, black locks had fallen as usual over his forehead. Azoff looked at him for a few seconds in silence; it was so natural and yet so strange to see him there, that perhaps at that moment he doubted the evidence of his senses.

"I have startled you," said Richard, in a gentle voice and with an indescribable smile. "I beg your pardon most sincerely," and he held out his hand and clasped that of Sergius. "I have been here twice to-day to find you, but the janitor told me you had gone out early this morning, and had not yet returned. I came the second time at eight o'clock, and I have been walking up and down the street to make sure of seeing you as you entered. A few minutes ago, I caught the glimmer of your light through a rent in your front window-curtain, and I knew you must be here. Either the janitor deceived me, or was deceived himself. I came upstairs without asking any more questions. You did not hear my knock at the door. I don't know why, but I had a suspicion of something wrong, and I came in without invitation. I have been waiting till you finished your letter, to speak."

"I am very glad to see you, Mr. Bayard," replied Sergius, with visible constraint.

"You are very glad to see me," repeated Dick, seating himself on the cot beside Azoff, "and yet you do not even ask a fellow, who tells you he has been walking up and down for two hours for the pleasure of seeing you, to take a seat."

Was it embarrassment, also, on Bayard's part, or the effort to conceal unwonted emotion, that made him talk so little like himself? The effort, if it were one, was not successful, and he began again rapidly in an altered, low, moved voice.

"Sergius Azoff I came to beg your pardon. In my thoughts, for many a day past, I have wronged you cruelly, but, thank God! not irretrievably, since I find you still here to receive my atonement. Do you know what it is that makes my heart go out to you to-night? It is that coarse, soiled, hideous garb which seems to me at the same time to desecrate and to sanctify the bravest and noblest man I have ever met. I came first to ask you to forgive me, and then to tell you that I should consider it the most singular good fortune of my life to be allowed the luxury of helping such a man."

And once again he extended his hand to Azoff, who clasped it long and warmly.

"I have never been mistaken in you, Richard Bayard," said the artist, after a pause. "But you are certainly in error about me. Why should I not speak frankly and freely to-night, if never again? Your suspicions were neither unfounded nor unjust. But your generosity now is based upon an altogether false idea of my qualities. This honest apparel is nothing but a masquerade costume. I have worn it for a day to cast it off forever. I am no more fit to wear it than I have been all my life to wear the garments of a prince. If it be this which commands your respect, take it back; I do not deserve it; I am a weakling and a fool."

He spoke in great excitement, and there was an unnatural gleam in his eye.

"You are neither one nor the other," said Richard; "you are an unhappy man. Life is so hard at times upon the strongest of us that we are apt to accuse ourselves of weakness because we faint and succumb. And yet I believe there is a remedy for all ills—but one."

"Which is, therefore, no ill," said Azoff, in a scarcely audible voice.

A sudden light flashed over Richard's face, but he made no answer.

"It is strange that you entered as you did," continued Mr. Azoff, hurriedly changing the conversation lest he should betray his purpose. "I was writing you a letter, which there is now no need to send," and in order to avert suspicion, he tore the note before him to scraps. "I wished to tell you about the night I met you in Waverley place. I was drunk,—besotted,—as I had been for many a night before with the same degrading poison."

"And as you have not been since, nor will be again, I think," said Bayard, calmly.

"How do you know that?" asked Sergius. "I make no pledges."

"The man who wielded the paving-ram on the high-road, this morning, was not an opium-eater," replied Dick.

"No, the opium-eater had fallen one degree lower," said Sergius, with a bitter laugh. "It was the merest accident that you saw me as you did this morning. I am neither a Saint-Simonist nor a common laborer. I have simply tried one more experiment in a life of experiments, and failed. I am used to that result now. Listen, Mr. Bayard. You are a man, I take it, of indomitable will,—of unassailable integrity. You are rich; you lead an honored, sheltered life. I should like to tell you the follies and miseries of a man who is adrift and isolated among his fellows; who, from no fault of his own, inherits a stigma which prevents him from meeting the eyes of his social peers; who is weak, who despises himself and who is hungry. Hold! not now," he added, with almost a smile, detaining by the arm Bayard, who half rose from his seat with a pained expression at the last words. "To-day I have earned my dinner. You saw me. I speak of the past month,—the previous six months. You are magnanimous, but it is not for that reason I consent to humiliate myself before you; it is because I feel the need to talk of myself freely and openly,—I am suffocating,—and because I am now past the reach of help or harm. I will begin at the beginning."

He paused, but only for an instant, and then went on slowly, thoughtfully, in that monotonous narrative tone with which men revive the emotions they have outlived:

"I have already told you that my mother was a famous artist. She was not married to my father. He was a Roumanian nobleman, one of the highest dignitaries of the state. I was a boy of thirteen when he deserted my mother. A short time after, we heard of his marriage with a lady of the court. I had been carefully brought up at home, away from boys of my own age, and had been kept in absolute ignorance of the stain upon my birth and the irregularity of my parents' life; now everything was revealed to me at once by a hundred voices, and I leave you to imagine the swelling torrent of indignation, grief and shame which overflowed my heart. I idolized my mother—no particle of blame then attached itself to her in my eyes,—nor ever has. Her love for my father was a passionate and a loyal one; it was the act of a coward to break the bond because no legal force had confirmed it; the burning desire of my heart for years was to avenge her wrong. As I grew older, I did not forgive him, but I recognized the fact that his sin was not one that could be punished by man, least of all by his own son. I hated, I scorned, I cursed him, but I met him face to face for years in the streets of Bucharest without even the desire to take the revenge I had vowed. When I was twenty years old he died.

"My mother has suffered cruelly from the wrong resulting from her own rashness; but I think I have suffered no less. Fancy a creature into whose veins has been transfused the blood of the poet and the aristocrat, sensitive at every pore, proud, passionate, ambitious, with a blight upon his birth, a jeer and a reproach connected with that which he holds most sacred,—his mother's fame,—a perpetual sneer as his greeting upon every face he meets. You have in this an explanation of my excessive ardor for republican principles, my extravagant idea of republican virtues.

"I have read somewhere that at the Devil's *Sabbat*, among all the elegant courtiers in their magnificent costumes, no matter how stately their bearing or how graceful their forms, there is always something about them, either too much or too little, which shocks the sense. They are a little too thin or a little too stout; a shade too pale or a shade too red; or suddenly a bird's claws or the inevitable cloven foot will appear inopportunely. I never could rid myself of the idea that I resembled one of these infernal gentlemen in my relations with the society to which my mother's genius and my father's rank should have admitted me. To all appearance I was one of that world, but the irremediable flaw was there, the cloven foot could not be concealed. In a word, in Europe there was no place for me, or, rather, I was wrongfully excluded from my proper place, and I resolved to come to America and, if possible, make my home here. Not that I desired any other companions than the artists who received me fraternally everywhere; but the constant sight and presence around me of the invidious distinctions of rank and caste and all the misery and meanness which they entail, continually stirred up the inexhaustible gall in my heart and made me unable to forget for a moment that I was a pariah.

"I came to America with brilliant, impossible dreams. Here I would work, here I would produce masterpieces, stimulated by the seething activity, the unhampered liberty, the splendid promise around me! You know what I found,—a place where a man who would live with beauty and art as his ultimate aim must feed on air and feast on moonshine,—who must be overwhelmed as a dreamer and a lunatic beneath the streaming tide of practical activities. There was no market for my pictures, and if I would gain a livelihood, I must fall into the ordinary business groove of the people who surrounded me.

"Nor was my only disappointment a purely personal one. The republican government which at a favorable distance seemed to me the simple reduction to practice of large and ennobling principles, I found on a nearer view, to be impeded by a hundred brawling political parties, corrupted by unscrupulous office-holders and attacked by still more unscrupulous office-seekers; the daily journals were filled with misgovernment in the cities, maladministration at the capital, abuse and obloquy heaped upon the central figure, I had pictured to myself as the most majestic and unimpeachable dignitary of all ages,—the President of the United States! And where were the republican equality and simplicity of manners I had dreamed? The standard of values was a little different, it had become one of fortune rather than of birth, necessarily in a country that had not yet seen its hundredth birthday. But that was all,—the same meanness, the same cringing, fawning snobbishness, a travesty of Old-World society,—the same ridiculous distinctions that even to a European seem ludicrous when conducted on so lilliputian a scale. The few intelligent elderly Americans with whom I had an opportunity of talking, scattered to the winds my darling political delusions. They who had lived longest under the existing institutions denounced universal suffrage as a failure, liberty of the press as an unbridled nuisance, invading the sanctity of men's most private affairs. Some went even so far as to advocate the abolition of the office of president and the substitution of a limited monarchy, or an electoral life protectorate. Richard Bayard, I would have cut off my hand rather than write home to my college comrades what I found in America!

"Nevertheless, I went bravely enough to work. I began to give lessons and lectures, with the hope of being able to earn enough to devote myself in time exclusively to producing, whether I sold my pictures or not. Alas! I found that the asphyxiated art-atmosphere, the tedious routine of monotonous grinding work were gradually paralyzing my productive faculties. Even when I had the leisure, I could not paint—my mind seemed stultified. I was constantly haunted by visions of young men of brilliant promise whose talent had prematurely exhausted itself. I grew morbidly distressed, and finally the idea of my incapacity became a monomania. I was in a fever from the moment I touched the brush. My hand trembled, and refused to obey my will. So this was the end of my lofty ambition—I had settled down into the fashionable drawing-master of New York! I grew impatient and indifferent toward my pupils, and gradually all—but one—fell from me. I deserved this, and accepted it doggedly. I had evidently miscalculated my stars when I fancied I was to remain a fashionable teacher. I was to be a beggarly artist starving in the streets. I actually suffered from hunger; I should have suffered from cold if the season had not been in my favor. When Mrs.—when my only remaining pupil paid me the amount of my last quarterly term, do you know what I did with it? I took it into a faro-house, laid it all desperately on a single stake,—and won! In one evening I gained double, treble, fourfold the amount of what I had worked away my soul for during the previous year. From that time I kept myself in a constant state of excitement with gambling and opium to forget my degradation and misery. The opium-eating ceased on the 16th of April,—it would have choked me after that. The gambling continued until my luck changed, and I lost everything I possessed but the clothes on my back. I passed two days sauntering through the streets—I think it was raining. In the afternoon of the second day,—that was yesterday,—I chanced to meet an artist friend, who asked me to dine with him. It was my breakfast, my dinner, my supper, for the previous forty-eight hours. Sandford had seen too much of Bohemian life, I fancy, to be surprised at my ravenous appetite. As we left the café, two burly Irishmen passed us by, and I heard one of them say, 'Damme! I had rather pound stones in the street than be dragged as low as that!' I almost felt as if he were talking to me.

"After my meal with Sandford I felt stronger and better than I had done for weeks. When I came home, I looked at myself with new eyes. In what respect was I different from that man who need never starve, nor beg, nor stoop to a vile act, while he had health and hands to wrest from the earth a livelihood? Anything would be better than the life I was leading now—a term of manual toil would only be carrying out the communistic ideas to which I had strongly leaned in my early youth. Well, I borrowed these clothes this morning, and I pounded stones on the road. Great God! With all my imagination, I never before realized the abject slavery in which millions of human beings are bound, to keep body and soul together. Yet even they cling to life, and wish to see the sun a little longer, as the saying goes. And as for me, I must wake up to the fact that even that brute, mechanical servitude was better than the use I had been putting my enlightened brain to for the past six months,—and, moreover, that even in this sphere there is no place for me, for Nature refuses to the effeminate bastard the power to dig and delve in her earth."

Azoff ceased. His whole figure and attitude suggested a hopeless dejection, with his elbows resting on his knees, his face supported by both hands, and his eyes blankly fixed in an ominous stare. Dick Bayard did not know how he could speak and at the same time suppress the painful emotion which swelled his heart to bursting. He felt that it was of far less importance at this moment to give vent to his sympathy (which was indeed sufficiently established by the fact of his presence and by his breathless attention to the artist's narration) than to maintain the firm yet gentle tone of authority which would enable him to preserve his beneficial ascendancy over this noble, unbalanced nature.

"There is but one use, Sergius," he said at last, with tolerable composure, "to which I never can believe in putting a human being, as long as he has a brain and limbs that need not be perverted to ignoble ends, and that is to shuffle him into a hole in the ground and shift the responsibility of his foibles on those who brought him forth, or those who some after and who must necessarily suffer for his loss. My ideas concerning life have been greatly influenced, no doubt, by the business community in which I have always dwelt. I do not consider it either a boon to be eternally grateful for, or a burden to be laid aside at pleasure. I consider it a difficult duty which has been imposed upon us without consulting our desire. The world seems to me an immense working-place,—a factory, if you will,—where each one of us has his special task assigned, which he cannot honorably shirk. A certain amount of labor has to be accomplished, for some universal end which we cannot conceive. The law is Progress; in generations we scarcely see a step of advance. *Eppure si muove!* The only cowardice I recognize is that of the man who doubles the work of his neighbor by deserting his post."

Sergius Azoff did not move.

"I have been listening to you," continued Dick, "with deep interest; but I must beg you in return to listen to me, even if I do not talk with quite so much eloquence. To begin as a patriotic American, I must tell you that there is one grain of wheat for twenty bushels of chaff in all you have rattled forth about America. The truth about this country lies just midway between the Utopian fancies you brought here, and the gloomy conclusions to which you have arrived now. You have made the common mistake of most Europeans of bringing the miniature standard of Europe with which to measure and judge a colossal experiment. In the first place, New York is not America, as Paris is France. Travel over the whole country from New York to San Francisco, from St. Paul to New Orleans, and tell me then that you have been disturbed by the Old-World prejudices of rank and caste. In the second place, you must learn to discriminate between the vulgar noise of a venomous world of ignorant politicians, and the grand, solemn, seldom-heard voice of the American people. It was the former that infested the presidency of General Grant with an infamous clamor of abuse; it was the latter which awarded to him, a second time, the highest honor in its power to bestow—the presidential chair. America is a country where art and beauty must and will thrive, though in the present transition period of upheaval and reconstruction, it is impossible to discern what forms they will assume. Wait until you have become better acquainted with the immense forces at work, with the gigantic scale on which the building of cities, the prosperity of a continent, the execution of divinely simple laws is conducted, before you write to your college-friends what is to be found in America. You were right," he went on with visibly increasing emotion, "in saying that Nature refuses a place to you among her delvers and diggers of the soil. Nature makes no mistakes; she does not create a sensitive, receptive brain, an accurate eye, an unerring touch, a poet's imagination, an ardent heart of universal sympathies, for the purpose of securing one more beast of burden. I thank God that you have failed to-day, Sergius Azoff, even though the failure has brought you to the brink of despair. I thank Nature that she has set her irrevocable fiat against degrading to servile uses the hand of the man I love."

Sergius Azoff did not speak, but he dropped his head and hid his burning face within his palms. Dick rose from his seat and moving toward him, laid his own hand gently on the artist's shoulder.

"Sergius," said he, " I came to ask of you a favor which you have not yet granted. Will you sacrifice your pride and condescend to accept help from me until you are better able to help yourself? Look at me,—we have talked out the night,—a new day is dawning."

Sergius started; a violent shudder passed through his frame. He rose and looked Richard full in the face; his eyes were moist, his cheeks were glowing, but his expression was firm and composed.

"You have saved my life," said he: "I lay it at your feet."

And in the gray light of the morning which broke in like a promise and an encouragement, the stately artist in his mean attire and the loyal-eyed American stood and clasped each other's hands.

EMMA LAZARUS *(1849–1887) is best known for her Statue of Liberty sonnet, "The New Colossus." During her brief life, she published five volumes of verse, including* Songs of a Semite; *a novel,* Alide: An Episode of Goethe's Life; *and numerous essays and poems in Jewish and general periodicals. "The Eleventh Hour" is her only short story. This is its first time in print since its initial appearance in* Scribner's Monthly *in 1878.*

VII. On Writers and Writing

Joseph Skibell

Willis Alan Ramsey & Me: A Bad Case of Second Novelitis

All I want to do is lie on the carpet and watch the sun move across the sky, tracking its path through the plate-glass windows of our living room, following it from the time it appears at dawn over my neighbor's house across the street until it slips behind our front eaves, lying perfectly still, sensing its presence above our roof, waiting for it to appear, hours later, over the back eaves, before it falls, at dusk, into the thicket of trees behind our house. If I could do this, I might be cured.

"Pay attention to the fantasies of healing in your patients," the psychologist James Hillman writes, "for often, therein, lies the actual cure."

It's good advice, I suppose, but I can't take it.

In the grips of a feverish and undiagnosed case of Second Novelitis (an ailment on which the DSM IV is silent), I can't permit myself the time. A harried sense of falling behind is the malady's prime symptoms: how can I lie on the floor all day when I have a second novel to write? *A second novel!* In the compendium of universal archetypes, is there a more blighted concept?) Lying on the carpet and doing nothing is the only thing that seems even *less* productive than the hours I spend each day at my desk.

"How's the new book going by the way?" asks a colleague of mine, a man who has no trouble turning out book after prize-winning book. Short stories, poems, novels, novellas fly out of him like ink from a leaky pen.

"Fine," I say. "If I could only remember the fundamentals of narrative, I might begin to make some progress."

The fundamentals of narrative.

Every morning, having failed to recall them to mind, I trudge dutifully to my desk anyway, where, like the Prophet Ezekiel contemplating the Valley of Dry Bones, I despair over anything returning to life. I don't understand the book I've begun. I can't remember how to describe a room or a face. My characters seem lifeless, their dialogue unfocused and inane. I've placed them in the desert of the southwest although the book's themes, as far as I can tell, has nothing to do with the desert or the southwest, and I don't know how to get them out of it again. Having used an old short story as a starting point, I can't maintain the prose style I employed only a few years before. Worse, I have no other ideas. Even worse, I know no matter how good the book might eventually become, it will never rival my first novel which feels to me, as the postpartum amnesia of its creation sets in, like an impossibly perfect jewel, a book that effortlessly wrote itself before going on to win a clutch of prizes and unanimous critical praise.

A part of me feels *finished* as a writer, *done*, as though I've paid off a longstanding debt, and I doubt I'll ever write anything again as satisfying or as meaningful.

"Of course you're blocked," says my friend Rick, when I complain to him, guiltily, about the consequences of my good fortune. He has yet to finish, much less publish, his own novel, and I feel like the narrator of a song I remember hearing during the Reagan era. Its four lines went: "I cried because I had no shoes/Until I met a man who had no feet./I said to him,/'Hey, can I have your shoes?'"

But Rick is sympathetic. He tells me about a study a psychologist devised. Having noticed that a group of kindergarteners, during their free period, all loved to play with the magic markers, he divided the class into two groups. Although the members of both groups could do whatever they wanted during the free time, the children in Group A were given graham crackers each time they played with the markers. When, after a while, the graham crackers were no longer given out as a reward for playing with the markers, Group A lost all interest in the markers, while Group B, the control group, continued playing with them as enthusiastically as before.

"You see what your problem is," Rick says.

"Not exactly, no," I say.

"You're in Group A. Not literally, of course. But the rewards of publishing might be effecting your writing in much the same way."

That's probably what happened to Willis Alan Ramsey, I think. Lately, I've been thinking a lot about Willis Alan Ramsey. When I'm not thinking about lying on the floor all day, I'm usually thinking about Willis Alan Ramsey.

Willis Alan Ramsey was an Austin songwriter who, in 1972, released a brilliant debut album called *Willis Alan Ramsey*. The record is to the ear what a cool beer and a tall woman in cut-offs and a tank-top on a hot summer day are to many of the other senses: a rapturously engaging aesthetic experience. If you were alive in the 1970s, you may still hear, as a memory in your inner ear, the pale cover versions of Ramsey's "Muskrat Candlelight," which, as "Muskrat Love," was a hit first for the group America and then, more anemically, for the Captain and Tenille. Recently, you may even have heard Jimmie Dale Gilmore's plaintive cover of "Goodbye, Old Missoula," but none of these would have prepared you for the rangy delights and the sheer wild-briar-patch musicality of *Willis Alan Ramsey*.

Wry, drawling, croaking, sly, seductive, innocently sincere, Ramsey's eleven performances, each better than the last, climax in a syncopated finale called "Northeast Texas Women." A paean to geo-graphically determined pulchritude ("...them Dallas women standin' up beat the others lyin' down..."), the song fades out at the end and fades back in for a brief coda. According to the liner notes, in addi-tion to guitars, fiddles and drums, the rhythm section here includes "bottle," "south wall," "coke crate," "knees," "cowbell," "carpet *&*

hallways." One by one, the instruments drop out, the music begins to disintegrate. A drumstick rattles. A guitar is tentatively plucked. Something that sounds like a Coke crate being dragged across a hallway and banged into a wall is indeed heard and then, as though he were predicting his own future, Willis Alan Ramsey announces in his twangy drawl, "Thay-is it."

And that *is* it.

Not quite forty minutes of music, it's all he's released over the last thirty-two years, despite shoals of critical praise, a well-financed tour, and a generous (although now thirty-two-year-old) advance from Leon Russell's (long-defunct) Shelter Recording Company.

"And so what?" I found myself reacting defensively against these thoughts and the self-pity they inspired. "So what if Willis Alan Ramsey never produces a second album? We're lucky to have one perfect album from him. Does the world really need a dozen middling others?" (Ramsey himself seems peevish on this issue. Asked by the *New York Times* what had become of his second album, he fired back, "What was wrong with the first one?") "And you're fortunate," I told myself, "to have written one satisfying novel. What law says you have to churn out book after book every two years?"

I remembered a Greek film student I knew in graduate school sighing over the year's paltry crop of films. "Where are this year's masterpieces?" he wondered glumly. "What's wrong with *last year's* masterpieces?" I chided him. "Isn't that the definition of a masterpiece, that it lasts for more than a year?"

And yet, I felt heartsick over my inability to write. What Rick had said about the kindergarteners seemed to apply only too accurately to me. In the beginning, writing had been a personal quest, an adventure in meaning, a way of emulating the authors whose work had meant so much to me. Now, it had become a career. It was like a dog I'd allowed to follow me home that I now had to take care of. And what once seemed like pleasurable daydreaming, especially to my mercantile family, was now a commercial venture that cast a real shadow in the world. The introverted practice of isolating myself in a room to arrange words on paper according to some idiolectic system had become a sales career, a shaky business venture that included conferences, meals out, airline reservations, public readings, interviews, autographs, articles, advertisements, and photo shoots. There were galleys to proof, blurbs to collect, journalists and bookstore owners to charm, jacket copy and cover art to approve. There were phone calls to return, book festivals to attend, letters to answer from readers, from editors, from agents, from admiring women, from other writers needing blurbs, advice, professional introductions. There were inquiries about adaptations, questions concerning translations, invitations to speak, to write, to teach, to travel, to explain.

And in this noisy, boisterous confirmation of my most privately cherished hopes for myself, the quiet, solitary work that produced it began to seem unbearably tedious and lonely. Sitting at my desk, staring at my empty notepads, tapping my pen against my teeth, I waited for the phone to ring, for the fax to whir, for an email to appear, for anything that might liberate me from the task of writing. Adding to my troubles was the fact that, though I couldn't quiet myself enough to write, I understood the continued health of this new career depended upon one thing only: the creation of a second novel.

I began to understand Willis Alan Ramsey's silence.

Having created a flawless first work, how was he supposed to start again from scratch, disappointing everyone with an album certain to pale in comparison? I'd already disappointed my editor. She so loved the first book that, one night in New York, after I'd given a reading from it, she mused aloud, in the cab we shared, how pleasant it would be if, instead of a second book, she could simply publish the first one again and again. "Who wants to read about a musicologist having a nervous breakdown in the desert, anyway?" she said, perhaps as a way of keeping down the advance my agent was negotiating with her. But when, as a dodge against confronting a second novel, I suggested I might write a collection of short stories instead, she was adamantly against it. "No, that would be a mistake. You've got momentum now as a novelist."

Momentum as a novelist was the only thing I didn't have.

Instead, what I had was a bad case of Second Novelitis which, as it metastasized, began to infect other areas of my life: I felt like a fraud, teaching creative writing to undergraduates in the job my so-called brilliant career had secured for me. Worse, I envied my students' ability to construct stories and scenes at my command. (Had I been enrolled in one of my own classes, I would have had to flunk myself.) I felt out of place in an English department, a fabulist among scholars, my MFA a pair of two's against the royal flush of their PhDs. I'd convinced myself that my colleagues were brilliant teachers, savvy theorists with a vast fund of critical knowledge and a complex inner life, which, in our anti-social department, they kept well-hidden from me. Things were worse in the Jewish Studies program, where, as an associate faculty member, I was the person for whom the others had to speak English, instead of Hebrew, during our meetings.

And yet, each day I continued to write, getting nowhere, rejecting ream after ream of tepid pages. I considered quitting my job, leaving my family, buying a boat, sailing to New Zealand. ("Burn down your house," a voice kept chanting in my ear.) Desperate, I retreated to an artist colony where I'd begun writing in earnest fifteen years earlier, but everything there seemed smaller and dirtier than I remembered it. The man who ran the colony was dead; his magnificent adobe house had fallen into humiliating disrepair. The fifteen years between my first stay and this one only accentuated how little I'd accomplished in the interim, and I still couldn't write. I spent a part of each day weeping on the floor.

As a more or less unsuccessful playwright and screenwriter, I'd spent years using rejection as a spur. (I once watched a play of mine while a woman in the row behind me kept whispering, "This is so stupid," to her husband, and felt nothing but a self-ironic sense of pride.) Hardened to criticism, I now found myself vulnerable to praise. It was as if my nervous system, having never encountered success, hadn't developed the antibodies necessary for fighting it off.

I wasn't alone. Willis Alan Ramsey and I weren't the only ones unable to face down the roadblocks thrown up by a successful first work. American literature is strewn with victims and near victims of Second Novelitis: Harper Lee, Marilynne Robinson, J.D. Salinger, and for thirty and sixty years respectively, Harold Brodkey and Henry Roth. A recent documentary about William Styron never even mentions his second book, the disastrous follow up to his highly praised debut. It's interesting to note that, in the wake of that disappointment, Styron produced his two masterpieces, whereas twenty-five years after the triumph of *Sophie's Choice*, his published fiction comprises fewer than half a dozen stories.

Clearly, failure is as essential as success for a long career.

Prolific writers like John Updike, Joyce Carol Oates, and Philip Roth, who churn out a book every two years, or compulsive film-makers like Woody Allen, may end up repeating themselves or even undergoing decades-long sloughs, turning out, for every masterpiece, three or four perfunctory pieces, but in the end, publishing steadily, they'll have created a large body of work which will more than likely contain the same small number of masterpieces as their less prolific, more circumspect peers.

I had lunch one day with Bruce Cockburn. Starting out three years earlier than Willis Alan Ramsey, he's produced over twenty-five albums since. He agreed with me that failure is necessary for a long career, but added that he didn't think it mattered if the failure was in your life or in your work. He'd had no trouble making another album after reaching a pinnacle with *Dancing in the Dragon's Jaws*, he said, but only because he'd gotten divorced immediately after it.

"There was nothing I could do *but* write songs."

Still, there'd been a stretch several years later when he couldn't write anything at all. Finally, in frustration, he gave up trying. Perhaps his career was over, he thought. He considered applying to art school, but after about eighteen months, he found himself sketching out a song he could stand and the albums that followed are among his strongest.

"Are you still working on that book?" a friend asks me.

Sheepishly I admit that I am.

"Do you have a deadline?" he wonders.

"Of course," I say.

"When is it?" he says.

"It was about two years ago, I think."

My fifteen minutes of literary fame are clearly over.

Following a British book tour and a paperback tour in America, the world finally forgets about me and my book. The hullabaloo dies down, the advance money runs out. I avoid talking to either my agent or my editor on the phone. There's nothing to do but return to the lonely life that awaits me at my desk every morning.

Eventually, I find myself, for the hundredth time, going over a scene I can't make work, when a small voice whispers in my ear, "You could cut that scene, you know, and end the section a scene earlier."

"Oh, no, I couldn't possibly do that," I say. "I couldn't possibly." I don't want to take time for any unexpected turns. I'm two years behind schedule, as it is, and though my plan for the book obviously isn't working, at least I have a plan.

"Try it," the voice is persuasive and reassuring.

Because it's a Friday afternoon, and my work week is essentially over, I decide to think about cutting the scene over the weekend and leave it at that. On Monday morning, when I come into my study, I stretch out on the floor hoping to be as relaxed as possible while I read over the pages. In this position, it's clear to me that the voice is correct. The scene is superfluous. In fact, there's only one sentence in it that I'd be sorry to lose. I make the decision to cut it and discover, to my delight that, when I have, the entire section, which I've been laboring over, takes on a new, dynamic energy, and suddenly springs to life.

After that, the rest of the book flows easily. Somehow, I understand what the story is about and how to move it forward.

When I'm almost done, I send a draft to a critic who has agreed to comment on my work as part of the academic tenure process. He'd given my first novel a rave in a major paper and I imagined he'd be a safe bet as an outside reviewer. I hardly know him and he isn't supposed to contact me during the review process, but one day he calls me at home to complain about the amount of material my university has sent him and also about the difficulty he's having getting a check from them for his work.

"And the only reason I agreed to do any of this," he grumbles, "was because I wanted to read your new novel."

Tensing up, I wait to hear what he might have to say about it.

"And?" I finally have to prompt him.

I stew nervously. It's a delicate moment, waiting for a comment like this.

"Well," he says, pausing, apparently reflecting, perhaps searching for the right word. "It's no *A Blessing on the Moon*, I'll tell you that. I mean, I couldn't really get into it."

My shoulders sink. I sigh.

I thank him. I tell him I'll look into the check.

I hang up the phone and I think: "Ah, at long last—sweet failure!"

JOSEPH SKIBELL's *first novel,* A Blessing on the Moon, *has won numerous awards and has been translated into half a dozen languages. His second novel,* The English Disease, *received the Jesse H. Jones Award from the Texas Institute of Letters. He joined the English Department at Emory University in 1999, and is working on a third novel, a collection of essays, a book of stories, a play and a collection of poems.*

Shaindy Rudoff

An Interview with Nava Semel

*I*n 1825, Mordecai Manuel Noah—an eccentric and controversial Jewish American diplomat, journalist, playwright, and Tammany Hall politician—completed the purchase of Grand Island in the Niagara River near Buffalo, New York. On September 15 of that year, a day after Rosh Hashanah 5586 (he made sure to note the Hebrew date) the flamboyant Noah declared the island "A City of Refuge for the Jews" and called it Ararat, nominating himself as "Judge in Israel."

The theatrical ceremony that accompanied the declaration caused quite a stir in Buffalo. But Noah's call to oppressed Jews around the world to settle on the island was ignored. No Jews arrived, and the enterprise was abandoned. Noah returned home to New York City.

Israeli writer Nava Semel's new novel revisits this obscure footnote in American history. One Sunday afternoon in June, I sat with the author in a café on Yehuda Hamaccabi Street in Tel Aviv. We discussed the novel, her unusual interest in Mordecai Noah, and her thoughts on Israel and America.

SR: Why don't you begin by summarizing the novel for the readers of *Maggid*.

NS: The novel, which I call in Hebrew *Ee-srael*, a combination of the words *ee* (which means both "island" and "not") and Israel, is divided into three parts. The first part opens in September 2001, when an Israeli named Liam Emanuel, a descendant of Mordecai Noah, inherits the deed to Grand Island and goes to America to claim his patrimony. He vanishes without a trace, and Simon T. Lenox, a police investigator of Native American descent, is assigned the task of finding him. Part Two goes back in time to 1825, to the week during which Ararat is dedicated by Mordecai Noah and in which, in the novel at least, Noah visits the island. Part Three is also set in 2001, only this time, in a world in which Noah's plan has succeeded—and Ee-srael has been a reality for almost two hundred years. The excerpt that you have here is the beginning of Part Two. It is the earliest chronological moment in the novel. The narrative here is told from the point of view of Little Dove, a young Indian woman who is a native of the island that has just been purchased for the Jews.

SR: Mordecai Manuel Noah was an amazing person—a secular yet traditional Jew of mixed Ashkenazi and Sephardi origins, a journalist, playwright, consul to Tunis, sheriff of New York, newspaper editor, orator, dreamer. Exactly what aspect of Noah attracted you to him?

NS: For me, Mordecai Manuel Noah is a prototype for Herzl. He was Herzl sixty years before Herzl. The resemblance is really striking. They're both journalists, they're both playwrights, which for me is very important. They are both people involved in international relations, and they both came up with the idea that the Jews need a safe haven. Because like prophets, they sensed a catastrophe somewhere.

SR: And even though they were both cosmopolitan people and accepted in their own right in the world, they were the ones to come up with the idea of a safe haven for the Jews.

NS: Right. And that's really interesting. For me, the striking resemblance is theater, and I even say this in the novel. Why is the vision of nation-building the enterprise of theater people? The whole notion of creating a land is the real drama. And maybe only theater people can envision or invent the whole concept of a Jewish land.

SR: Have you read any of Herzl's or Noah's plays?

NS: Herzl wrote one good play—*The New Ghetto.* Noah wrote a series of plays that are very American, very patriotic and sentimental. I can't imagine them being produced today.

SR: How did you find out about Mordecai Noah in the first place?

NS: That was very strange. When I was a child in the sixties I received the gift of a book—I think I got it for my bat mitzvah. It was a collection of incredible events in history. And I remembered reading something about a Jew who created a Jewish homeland—or something like that. It was planted in my head a long time ago and I forgot all about it. When I was living in America, I was at the New York Public Library, researching something I was working on at the time. And I came across a reference—a footnote in something that mentioned Noah and Ararat—and it clicked from my childhood. And I immediately knew that I had found a lost treasure. I remember how it hit me in the New York Public Library, and I knew it was something I would research. And I researched it for about ten years. In the meantime, I wrote seven other books. Because I knew that I wanted to deal with the issue of Ararat, but I didn't want to write an historical novel. There was an historical novel written about Mordecai Noah in the year that I was born—in 1954—by Yochanan Twersky. I have a copy, probably the only copy that exists. And it's a very Zionist novel, saying, no—Ararat didn't succeed, only Zion.

For me it was incredible to discover that the concept of the Jewish state predates Herzl. Here I was, an Israeli kid who knew the

Zionist narrative, or who believed she knew it, and all of a sudden I discovered something had been censored. I think it was the preference of the Zionist narrative not to acknowledge the fact that there had been an option in America. It's not so comfortable. Better to start the Zionist narrative with Herzl and make Uganda the failed option. But to think that there might have been something before Herzl, and that we could have gotten there easily…I think that, subconsciously, the story of Ararat was swept under the rug. So the discovery that it exists was a real revelation for me and a great opportunity to re-examine the Zionist enterprise.

sr: Obviously, Part One and especially Part Three are flights of the imagination. But even in Part Two, you don't feel bound by historical fact.

ns: I see history as a trampoline. I don't want to go back into the past just to recreate the past. What's interesting to me is to recreate the present, not the past. And what really excites me is to speak about the future. But it's wrapped in the disguise of the past.

According to all my research, Noah never stepped foot on Grand Island. So I decided to take him there secretly. I forced him to set foot there. I was really offended by my research. I was angry at him. I threw my papers at him and said—what is this? You bought a piece of land for the Jews and never went to see it?

The narrator, Little Dove, is the last Indian person on the island. It is the night before the inauguration ceremony for Ararat. According to tradition, the island is hers. Legally, it already belongs to the Jews. But she wants to take Mordecai Noah to the island to show him that he hasn't bought an empty island. That there's no such thing as an empty place. Because the air is full of spirits and full of ghosts and full of special plants, etc. The Jews—they are going to come to a place that will force them to change their way of viewing the world. And this is something that I say not just about Indians and Jews. I say it about the Palestinians and the Israelis, too. Zionism was blinded by its own concept that this was a vacant land.

Part Three is a flight of the imagination. It imagines the world with an Ee-srael that has succeeded. Rather than becoming a laughing stock with the project collapsing, the Jews come. And this is the most interesting investigation for me as an Israeli, because here I neutralize the three most significant components of the Israeli psyche and identity. One, there's no Holocaust; two, there's no Arab-Israeli conflict; and three, no Hebrew language.

But even though Part Three is most unbound by history, I actually change as little as possible in terms of history. Hitler does come to power in 1932. The change is that, since Ee-srael already exists, a convoy comes to Europe to collect all the Jews. There is a holocaust of homosexuals, cripples. But the Jews have been plucked out. And September 11th still happens. In fact, all of the chapters take place between September 9th and 15th Part Two in 1825, and Parts One and Three in 2001.

SR: The Holocaust, the Arab-Israeli conflict and *Hebrew?*

NS: Oh yes. The revival of Hebrew is one of the great success stories of the twentieth century. And I realize that most American Jews haven't experienced that. That's why I want them to come here—at least once. There is something in Israel that you have to experience if you are a Jew. You are forced to confront your Jewish identity with Israeliness. Hebrew is a big piece of this.

When I lived in New York I felt the confrontation between Bavel and Jerusalem. I sensed that New York Jews felt that they were at the center of the Jewish world. The truth is that the most exciting Jewish cultural things are done in Hebrew. In 1990, I had a terrible argument with Joseph Papp. My husband and I went to an evening that he organized in New York—an homage to Yiddish. It was narrated by Meryl Streep, a WASP, William Hurt, a WASP. I didn't mind that they were doing a tribute to Yiddish to raise money for YIVO. But Hebrew wasn't even mentioned as a phenomenon. It was presented as if the Jews of Western Europe moved to America and Yiddish came with them and in between...nothing happened. Neither was the State of Israel established, nor was the Hebrew language revived. And I was freaking out. I wrote Papp a letter. I wrote him, "We fuck in Hebrew and we die in Hebrew." He never invited us to anything after that.

I think now that this experience of a Jewish world that could imagine itself without Israel and without Hebrew had a big impact on my imagination. Perhaps that was the moment when this book was born. In the novel there's a couple that says, "Let's make love in Hebrew—from right to left. And let's die in Hebrew." That's a clear trace of the Papp incident.

SR: The real Mordecai Noah believed that the American Indians were descendants of the Lost Tribes of Israel. This was a way to lay claim to ancient Jewish origins in America. Did this come into play for you?

NS: It's a very nineteenth-century romantic notion. But first of all it gave me the opportunity to have Noah have a love affair with an Indian woman. She also becomes pregnant. I give him two lines of descendants: one line of children in Israel, and one line—an Indian line—in America. His great grandchildren will no doubt kill me!

SR: So he's like a Jewish Thomas Jefferson.

NS: Yes! I loved the idea that he believed in the lost tribe theory because even though it's romantic and even though it's considered today to be ridiculous, the notion of a multiracial world is very modern. When you say that the Indians are the descendants of the lost tribes, you have to take into account that they will bring with them what they have acquired along the way. It's not just that we will convert them. That's not it. It's that we will accept the gift of who they were. That's a modern notion, and this I really liked and wanted to use. In the novel, the Indians are the first refugees in Ee-srael. Instead of being deported south—on the "trail of tears"—many of them come to the island. The Jews open their state to them.

SR: So the Native American characters in the book function as a way for you to open up questions of racial and ethnic identity.

NS: All of my characters ask, What's the difference between Jews and Israelis? In order to ask these questions, my novel deals with encounters of Israelis, and Jews, through the eyes of non-Jews, non-Israelis. Simon T. Lenox and Little Dove are Native Americans who watch Jews, who track Jews. She is touched by the fact that they chose an Indian island as their final destination.

SR: Is she touched or threatened?

NS: Both. It's her choice to give the island with no bloodshed. But she has to fight with her own ancestors who come as spirits in her head and tell her, Kill the Jew. Blow up the island, so that no one will have it. It takes a lot of energy for her to overcome the instinct to destroy him and the island and give away the island in a peaceful way.

I realize, of course, that this is controversial because I seem to be implying that the conquered must accept their situation peacefully. Is peaceful behavior the only justifiable solution?

A few generations later, Simon T. Lenox is very much taken with the idea of "what if." If we could change history and could have created a Jewish state within the United States, could it have created a different racial reality that would have educated the American public differently, not just for Jews—but for Indians, and for all other races? So even my Indian is taken with the question of "what if?" The whole book is caught up, in essence, with the question of "what if."

In Part Three, I have other non-Jewish perspectives as well. The narrator is a black paparazzo whose lover is a native born Ee-sraeli.

SR: America means a lot of different things to different people. What is America to you?

NS: I need to answer this on two personal bases. Part of my yearning for America is that it is partly home for me. I had an American grandfather. I might easily have been an American Jew. Had history been changed—had my father agreed to go with my grandfather in 1946—I would have been born in New York. Secondly, my twin children were born in America. And I always feel a debt to America. America enabled me to have two more children. In Israel the technology wasn't that advanced at that time. I grew up with a grandfather who always told me that America is the promised land of the Jews. That the Jews have no future in Israel. He thought that this experiment in the Middle East would end in disaster. And I was a Zionist girl who opposed what he said very strongly. It was very hard for me to accept as a child. But it could be that, as I grew up, there's been something in me that has been checking out that other alternative. It's clear that I have deep sentiments for America. It's not a strange place for me. I have "heimish" feelings because of my grandfather and my "American" children, I feel the bond. Something very intimate happened to me via the American voyage. Nevertheless, I am an Israeli. I would never choose another place. It's not even a matter of choice. I am the byproduct of Israel and Zionism. For better and for worse. I acknowledge it. The only place where I allow myself to have doubts, to exile myself, to imagine myself without Israel or Hebrew is through my writing. It has been a rollercoaster. And there have been no definite answers.

SR: How do you understand the kind of crisscrossing of desires—of Americans for Israel and Israelis for America—that is so prevalent and powerful today?

NS: There is a metaphor in the book called Damascus vs. New York. The one who lives in New York wants to live in Damascus, for him Damascus is a remote place where he can find tranquility, a break from the ambition and viciousness of the urban center. That's his *shummakom*—his elsewhere. But the one who lives in Damascus hates Damascus. It's a boring, provincial corner of the universe and he wants to be in New York—a metaphor for everything exciting, the place where everything happens. In the book, Simon T. Lenox stops on the road between New York and Grand Island at the Damascus Diner. The road takes him from Goshen to Liberty. It takes forty-five minutes to get from Goshen to Liberty. In the Bible it took a lot longer. And he sits in the Damascus Diner realizing that everyone always wants to be somewhere else.

The Jews are champions at wanting something that doesn't exist. That's true. They are fascinated by "the promise." Abraham got a promise. And on the basis of that promise, they moved and moved and moved for thousands of years. And the question is whether they want the promise to be realized. It could be that the best thing for the Jews is to chase after the promise and never realize it. Because then the disappointment is so great. I only know that I like the journey. Ultimately, I am an Israeli. So there's no *shummakom* for me. I may criticize Israel. I may complain and whine about it all day long. But there's no other place for me. In the novel, after his encounter with Liam Emanuel and the Grand Island affair, Simon T. Lenox decides to resign from his job and change his life. His dialogue with the Israeli has convinced him not to give up on the idea of a home.

SHAINDY RUDOFF *teaches American literature and directs the Creative Writing Program at Bar Ilan University.*

Nava Semel

The Island of Israel

I was never taught how to track Jews.

From the moment I was born under the roaring waters, Father Raven, you made me aware of the signs. *Pay attention, Little Dove, to the break among the ferns. A white-tailed deer bounded there on its way to drink. A falcon took flight from atop the white oak; a bunch of leaves fell on your head. A beaver rose up from the river, leaving the imprint of its fur caressing the earth's skin.*

They have all gone, yet they remain. For they leave tracks. The world as it is, and the world as it was. I can see both. But I cannot track Jews. For them, you gave me no signs in any world.

I can see before me now, that which came before what came before. My small palm is in your hand, Father Raven. You bring it close to the trembling line of the river's edge, but you stop me from separating earth and water. Then you plunge my hand, as if it had been cut off, but without pain. I was not afraid. I trusted my Father Raven.

Our own tracks were also planted on the banks of the Niagara on that faraway day, if anyone had bothered to look for us. The prints of a man's moccasins and the bare feet of a little girl. At that time I did not understand the mysteries of tracking, why parents were so committed to them and why children were required to learn them so well. As we left the bank, you pointed out the violently snapping tail of a black mullet who accidentally leaped on shore.

I said, "Not even a fish would surrender its place without a fight." And you noted in me the tracks of a white thought.

I asked whether the spirit would still nestle in him when he returned to the water, and you laughed. I questioned no further. I had known then so few suns and moons.

Human beings, pale-skinned and red alike, build barriers between themselves and the earth, defying the knowledge that one day they will be forced to return to it. This I say now, Father Raven, many suns and moons after you have departed for the eternal hunting grounds. In your absence, I have had to probe the mysteries alone, to follow in the void the spear no senses can perceive, and tonight the powers have brought my way these unfamiliar tracks. A Jew chief sails in a canoe carved by my own hands, and the weight of his body slows the journey. He will wound the earth and leave his strange scent. For no member of his tribe has ever tread upon this place. Or else, the winds long ago have carried his scent elsewhere.

We sailed from Buffalo, a frontier settlement of whites whose lights encroach upon our rear. A temporary place in my eyes, though permanent in the eyes of my mistress, Mrs. Lenox.

Even if I would extinguish my eyes, the waterway would open for me, for this river knows me better than I know myself.

I rowed in the darkness, and the Jew chief cast his glance toward the black horizon, scouting like a blind man for some shape in the landscape, failing to notice the approaching shore.

I had pity on him: "We'll be there soon. Don't you trust me?"

In the chief's silence I discern tracks of fear. Huddling in his coat and continuing to glare into the darkness, like one of our boys, setting out alone on his coming-of-age journey. But he is not a boy; he is a man, and he has sailed the seas and seen the world. Six days, the guest sat in Mistress's splendid parlor and recounted his tales, and all the grandees of Buffalo gathered around him with gaping eyes and mouths.

On this night, the seventh since his arrival, he holds on to the side of the canoe like a cradle. Perhaps he is afraid I will deliberately drown him, or maybe his tribe has never seen a woman navigating.

I said to him: "The Great Spirit will guide us." I did not say: "Your bones are resting there, Father Raven, waiting for their final burial, trusting that I will someday observe the tribe's custom."

You are the last. Guard our bird-shaped island, embraced by the arms of the Niagara.

Tomorrow the island will pass into the hands of its new owners. With paper money, the Jew chief bought it from the authorities, and when the sun rises, he will declare it the legal property of his tribe and call upon them to come here.

There are many islands in the world other than this little bit of dirt jutting into the sloping river. This is no great sea, no glory-seeking ships explore its mysteries. But to me, an island-home, my whole world. To the chief of the Jews it is nothing at all, a small patch scratched with a quill on a scroll of paper the whites call "maps." Without them, they cannot take a step anywhere. But the real tracks are not marked on a piece of paper. The meadow turning gold in the summer and the rustling canopy of leaves heralding autumn. Coyotes, raccoons, wild geese, doves and ravens, all move in their circles, under maple trees and elms. Everything in its place, as if there is no Buffalo, no America. This island alone exists. His chosen island. My imposed heir. Had I not insisted on bringing him here, he would not have stepped foot here at all.

We are approaching the cove, and I offer to help the Jew chief get out of the rolling canoe, but he declines my outstretched hand, slips going from water to land and hurriedly tries to get up. If we were the same size, I would give him my beaded moccasins and go barefoot. But he is a big man and I am just a little dove.

He did not even ask my name, though he announced his twice, lest I get it wrong. I looked for markings of a chief on him. No multicolored feathered headdress, and none of those metal tokens that the palefaces adorn themselves with after a battle.

I said, "Welcome." He answered: "In whose name do you greet me, woman? This island in uninhabited."

Are the senses of the Jew chief impaired? Does he not perceive the island's inhabitants, stirring in the foliage, in the water, in the earth. How can he lead his tribe here, if he is unable to follow the tracks? And how can I teach him the mysteries and signs in one night?

I steady the stern of the canoe on the shore, while the rest of it hugs the water. In case of danger, I will quickly be able to row back. I place the paddle, smooth and slippery as a fin, on the bottom of the canoe and pack up the mat that protected my knees while rowing. The Jew chief is haughty, and the blot of his paleness flickers in the darkness that envelopes the island.

Of all the possible homelands in the world, why did my lowly, grassy island have to be chosen? What does the chief of the Jews have to do with this out-of-the-way piece of land?

Arriving at Mistress's estate, he brandished a deed of purchase. For a minute, I thought he was just fanning the air, but he kept insisting that he held in his hand a valuable possession, a rare treasure.

Mistress turned to me: "You were born there, no?" Yet she did not wait for an answer.

Mistress's husband took the deed of purchase, rubbing it with his fingers, the same way he inspects the silver-gray fur of a grizzly bear and bargains with the Inuit hunter who comes from beyond the Great Falls. "You're a lucky man, Major Noah. You know how to pull the right strings." Then he winked, "You Jews"—as if he were saying, "You Indians."

Yet the chief is white like them.

"Earth is not property. It is given to all creatures for safekeeping." I dared voice a red thought, and the men in the parlor in Buffalo laughed. Their laughter rolled like barrels.

"Land is merchandise, girl, just like the corn you help us grow. And in return, we generously provide you with protection. This is a new world, and there's a law of supply and demand. But you wouldn't understand. How much did you pay, Major Noah? Jesus, a real bargain. Had I known that nearby Grand Island was for sale...."

Then he began to walk back and forth in the parlor, calculating.

"Maybe there are other places on the market," Mistress suggested, and even raised the idea of a liquidation sale. "There must be a place where no man would want to live or die, some island prison, like Elba or Saint Helena, where ten years ago the deposed Emperor Napoleon was exiled."

Again the men's laughter echoed in the parlor in Buffalo.

Suddenly, Mistress's husband tensed. His white thought paled even more. His eyes hurled a tomahawk toward the Jew chief, and he said, "So close by—an island of Jews."

He turned, and I saw right away that he was reaching for his musket.

It was then I told the Jew chief: "I will take you there."

An island prison.

An island of exiles—

What are Jews?

Don't Father Raven and Little Dove have the right to know who are their heirs?

—*Translated by Michael P. Kramer*

Born in Jaffa, Israel, NAVA SEMEL *has published eleven books and three plays, both for adults and children, including* Becoming Gershona, *which received the 1990 National Jewish Book Award, and most recently,* The Rat Laughs. *The recipient of numerous awards, among them the 1996 Israeli Prime Minister Award for Literature, her work has appeared in the* USA, *Germany, Italy, the Czech Republic, Spain, Austria, Holland, England, France, Romania and China.* Ee-srael *will be published in Hebrew in 2005.*

Paul Zakrzewski

First Loves and Other Sorrows

First Loves by Ted Solotaroff (Seven Stories, $24.95)

Coming of age in the late 1940s, Ted Solotaroff is a bundle of contradictions and divided loyalties. At home, he acts as the buffer between a needy, sensitive mother and an emotionally abusive, estranged father. At college—half way across the country, as far as he can get from New Jersey—he daydreams about becoming a radical labor lawyer, but has only a tenuous grasp on the politics of the time. Naïve enough to assume that his Navy experiences with prostitutes will help to guide him in romantic love; he's nonetheless able to fool some of the women in his life. Worse still, he longs to create in his fiction the distant, formal cadences of Joyce, and the cool attitude of Hemingway, but ends up with only stilted imitations. This is as much the result of his misguided desire to emulate the modernist masters (and leading anti-Semites) of his day—squandering the rich legacy of his Jewish upbringing—as it is his inability to accept his genuine inclinations towards literary criticism.

How Solotaroff reconciles these contradictions, navigating his way through his turbulent twenties, is the subject of his second full-length memoir, *First Loves*. At its best, his writing captures with nuance and a striking degree of understanding the theme of all good autobiographical writing: the process by which we become ourselves, reconciling our past and present, our ambitions and limitations. He does so by offering the story of two deeply entwined desires, the titular "first loves."

The one is quite literally so, a tempestuous romance with Marilyn (or Lynn) Ringler. It is 1948 as the memoir opens, and the twenty-year-old Solotaroff watches as the mysterious Lynn emerges Venus-like from the ocean. They flirt a little over her likeness to Natasha in *War and Peace*, but she seems otherwise aloof and uninterested. The ambitious but ungainly Solotaroff scores better with some of the other student intellectuals who meet on the beach to discuss Edmund Wilson and Marxism. But Lynn is not as unattainable as she first appears. As it turns out, she, like Solotaroff, is working for the summer at Lido Beach, New Jersey, scraping together money for her freshman year. Furthermore, they share a similar hardscrabble urban Jewish upbringing, and are both off to Michigan in the fall; he to Ann Arbor, she to neighboring Michigan State (Lynn, ever the New Yorker with no sense of geography between the oceans, mistakes the less prestigious school for the University of Michigan).

While his love for the beautiful but deeply mercurial Lynn is kept in check, his desire for a life of writing and literature grows. At Michigan, his advisors quickly steer him past his vague notions of becoming a lawyer, getting him hooked on the Greek classics instead. He learns even more from fellow classmates, who challenge his flimsy politics (he supports John Dewey but doesn't seem to understand why). But the hardest lessons of all are the ones he learns from experience: like the time an instructor confronts him with the fact his true talents may not lie with fiction, but criticism. Comparing Solotaroff's stilted stories to those of student writers, the instructor pulls no punches: "'They trust their imagination completely, its individuality, its grasp. The trust is a kind of primal thing that goes deeper than technique, deeper than words, even deeper than talent.... You, on the other hand, don't trust your imagination and have to rely on others. What you do trust completely is your literary judgment and insight, which is why your judgments are bold and your insights keen, sometimes even original…'"

It is the discovery of his Jewish self that fuels Solotaroff's evolution from fiction writer manqué to literary critic. Admittedly a product of his time, the young man holds the decidedly non-Jewish modernist critics of the day in the highest esteem, an act that "separated for a long time my interests and values as a fiction writer from my upbringing, my felt past; the writer I wanted to be from the person whose core was still middle-class Jewish." He may be understandably eager to put his difficult days in New Jersey behind him, but as with his friend Philip Roth, this background provides the source and power of his writing. He discovers, to his surprise, that he understands, intimately understands, the fictional landscape of the writers he loves, Malamud, Roth and Bellow. Their past is not so different from his. With the help of Jewish critics such as Irving Howe and Leslie Fiedler, he recognizes that these writers represent a new day in American Jewish writing. His seminal 1959 essay "A Vocal Group," recounted here in fascinating detail, helps to place these writers in a fresh context. The conflict between the uncouth and refined (Roth) and the process of self-discovery through suffering (Malamud and Bellow) echo Solotaroff's own struggles—one reason why he is able to articulate so strikingly these writers' accomplishments.

Elsewhere, *First Loves* is filled with an impressive roster of meetings with remarkable men (yes, mostly men). Bernard Malamud, Norman Podheretz, Leslie Fiedler, Isaac Rosenfeld, Dylan Thomas, as well as a young Philip Roth, are only a few of the literary greats who parade through these pages. Nevertheless, the most complex relationship continues to be the one the young man has with Lynn, and—as befits a muse who emerges from the ocean—she alternately inspires and bedevils him. Eventually, Lynn and Ted get married, have babies, and shuttle between Michigan, New York and Chicago. But if the pair share interests outside the bedroom, then they appear entirely mismatched within. The scene of their first tryst makes for painful reading, but Solotaroff's ability to record the conflict between his early needy self, and Lynn's anger with his lack of finesse, is expertly drawn. Underscoring one of the potential pitfalls of memoir-writing, however, the book veers between a sensitive portrayal of the couple's dysfunction and one that's pointlessly explicit. (In an odd moment, Solotaroff recalls, apparently without irony, how he recoiled at "all the ugly physical detail" in Philip Roth's story "Epstein". "Why all the *shmutz*?" he asks the author, to which Roth snaps back, "The *shmutz* is the story.")

Yet the couple's sexual problems seem to pale next to the psychological ones: Lynn struggles with depression, mood swings, and hallucinations. Teasing one minute, she grows cold and distant the next. Perhaps enacting Solotaroff's own unresolved feelings about Lynn, her story is, by turns, an engaging and frustrating one. For the first part of the memoir, she is an enchanting character, teasing her suitor as she holds him at bay. For much of the story, however, Lynn comes across as little more than a major nuisance. Though there's something clearly alienating and difficult about their love, he never seems to be able to get into her head, and she remains bafflingly child-like and unsympathetic in this depiction.

A further weakness in the memoir is the writing itself. When he is making literary judgments or capturing his own evolution as a critic, Solotaroff's writing shines with the born essayist's clarity and grace. Yet many of the scenes and characters in between these moments seem hastily drawn, as if their creator were anxiously rushing to the next bit of analysis, the next literary judgment. Indeed, *First Loves* suggests that Solotaroff's real strength lies elsewhere—for example in his essays and reviews, such as those collected in the stellar anthology *A Few Good Voices In My Head*. It is notable that a couple of the most effective sections in *First Loves* actually first appeared as personal essays—for example, "Silence, Exile and Cunning" (in which becoming a father is linked to giving up fiction writing and returning to graduate school), or "Driving Bernard Malamud" (a hilarious yet ultimately sobering vignette of the time Solotaroff chauffeured the deceptively staid writer around Chicago in his rusted-out car). In these essays, Solotaroff captured his youthful foibles with vigor, even as he subtly teased out the larger social, literary, and emotional concerns. By contrast, many sections of the memoir appear loose and baggy, a little too breezy to move and surprise the reader.

Though the memoir ends in the early 1960s, as his first marriage dissolves, we know the rest of the story. Before retiring a few years ago, Solotaroff went on to have a successful career as an editor and critic at some of the most respected journals (*Commentary*) and publishing houses (Harper *&* Row, now HarperCollins) in the country. His breakthrough came in 1967, when he was asked to edit *New American Review* for New American Library. Under his stewardship, the magazine eschewed any school of fiction, poetry or criticism, citing only "taste" and "freshness" as a guide. In the editor's note accompanying the first issue, one detects the same man whose battles with modernism and other reigning orthodoxies animate his memoir. In the note, he wrote: "We are more interested in publishing writers who are arriving than those who are departing or standing still." In many ways this philosophy could serve as a summary of his career, too. As the memoir ably reveals, Solotaroff got beyond his early sorrows to make his mark as a champion of the new, the smart, and the underappreciated. Perhaps it's fitting then that the best moments of *First Loves* are the ones that capture the transformation.

PAUL ZAKRZEWSKI *is a writer and critic based in Boston. He is the editor of* Lost Tribe: Jewish Fiction from the Edge *(HarperCollins), and his writing has appeared in* Time Out New York, The Forward, *and elsewhere.*

Marshall E. Wilen

Out of Place

The Place Will Comfort You by Naama
Goldstein (Scribner, $23)

> *May the Lord [lit., place] comfort you among*
> *the other mourners of Zion and Jerusalem.*
> —Traditional condolence

Jewish literature has long been thought of as the literature of the
outsider, of the stranger in a strange land. But I have always had
a naïve faith that the alienation of the Jew was as much a condition
of place as of nature. In a Jewish homeland, Jewish writers could
finally kick loose of that annoying preoccupation with not belonging, freeing themselves to obsess about other subjects—eros, religion,
politics, survival.

As Naama Goldstein's highly original, elliptical, and demand-
ing short stories present the contemporary Israeli experience, I was
mistaken. This ironically titled collection, *The Place Will Comfort You*,
illustrates that the wandering Jew may have found a home in Israel,
but she hasn't necessarily found a place.

The Place Will Comfort You is Goldstein's debut as a writer,
one in which she defines for herself a unique position as chronicler
of a multicultural Israeli community in which no one feels quite

"absorbed." As Rabbi Haziza in the story "Barbary Apes" explains, "our community did not spring up out of the Rock fully formed"; we are all "travelers...exiles," even in our own land.

Rising from Goldstein's own background as the daughter of American *olim* who returned to the United States when she was in high school, this "split perspective," as the author called it in a recent interview (on *JBooks.com),* both energizes and haunts her stories and enables her to capture characters who inhabit a precarious middle ground between belonging and alienation, Orthodoxy and secularism, rebellion and conformity, childhood and womanhood.

This is not a comfortable place, the reader quickly realizes.

In the opening tale, "The Conduct for Consoling," an American-born schoolgirl is selected to represent her class in a shiva call to a classmate. The most finely-pitched piece in the collection, the story follows the unnamed child (could she be the Shulee of the later tales?) as she visits the "Orphan," a Sephardi girl of lesser means but freer spirit who insists on becoming the protagonist's friend. Goldstein shows her character's emotional confusion as she confronts their cultural and class differences, the meaning of grief and loss, and the enticing but frightening freedom that her friend's orphanhood bestows.

In "Pickled Sprouts," a fifth-grader feels embarrassingly out of step with her classmates because of her American parentage. She drinks milk, not coffee; she's not extroverted like the sabras; she carries an American-style metal lunch box that marks her foreignness for all to see. "It is as if you were raised somewhere very different, then put down here," she moans, despite being born in Israel. When she's assigned to help in the school kitchen, she discovers an unlikely ally in the cook, a heavily-accented grandmotherly Holocaust survivor who asks, "What is this culture from? This pushing and this shoving."

Mr. Durchshlag, in "The Verse in the Margins," teaches Jewish studies in a religious vocational school for girls. A "veteran" who finds every excuse to remind his charges how he served his country as a member of the army's Holy Society preparing dead soldiers for burial, he sees himself as his students' guardian against secular influences. So much so that he becomes outraged when his favorite student—"a good girl...not like the others"—appears in school sporting immodestly garish earrings. Humiliated, the girl runs away from the school. Durchschlag rushes out to retrieve her and winds up descending into a Tel Aviv version of Nighttown, where he finds a strange kind of penance, if not redemption.

"A Pillar of Cloud" offers a more light-hearted illustration of the cultural divide. A cousin from Connecticut invades the home of an Israeli family and shakes things up in unexpected ways. Brash, uncouth, and annoyingly irrepressible, the visitor—an optician who brings a suitcase full of optical equipment with her—opens the children's eyes in more ways than one. When she invites an Arab handyman over for dinner, what began as comedy slyly transforms into a double-edged comment on the American's naïveté and the Israelis' prejudice.

Goldstein's young protagonist comes into her teen years in "The Roberto Touch," revealing all the promise and self-destructive willfulness that comes with the adolescent territory. During a class field trip, Shulee pulls a selfish prank that lands her and a friend in a situation that quickly changes from humorous to genuinely dangerous.

These stories comprise the first section of the book, entitled "Olim (Ascending)." The stories in the "veYordim (and Descending)" section are more "adult" and less fully conceived. "Anatevka Tender," "Barbary Apes," and "The Worker Rests Under the Hero Tree" all feature adult protagonists who have "descended" to the United States. In each, the return to the States is fraught with disappointment, guilt, and a sense of failure. "Anatevka Tender" explores the guilt and anger that wracks a mother who has brought her family back from Israel just a bit too late: her eldest son has already been irretrievably damaged by his Army service. In "Barbary Apes," a young woman in an Orthodox women's college gets a barbed lesson in Jewish history from her professor, an exotic Sephardic rabbi from Gibraltar.

"The Worker Rests Under the Hero Tree" shows Goldstein at her most ambitious as she portrays the tentative emotional dance between two lonely expatriate Israelis lost in gentile New England. Adi is working as a caregiver to a severely handicapped young man in a small town in a "half-wild strip of Cape Cod" when she comes across a familiar name in a local newspaper article: that of Neer Shabazi, the former neighbor who once rescued her from a child molester when she was seven. Hopeful and excited, she arranges to meet her hero. Their meeting, fraught with expectation, hope, and irresolution, becomes a darker adult mirror of the dilemmas facing Goldstein's younger characters in the earlier stories.

But this story, along with its companions, also illustrates the challenges and limitations of Goldstein's writing. She seems to have sought a linguistic correlative to the emotional distance of her subjects, and at times she seems to have found it. Witness this example of Goldstein at her most lyrical:

> She [Adi] had gone through so much before happening on this [coming across her savior's name in the newspaper].... At last she felt peace. Neer Shabazi, here where she lived now. A morning breeze blew through the kinked venetian blinds, scented of seaweed. Birds had awakened in the walnut and were agitating for activity.... Neer, here where she was now, this peaceful place, this cape of cod.

But then we come across such befuddling phrases as "the man was simply unable to cull theories of personal intention from the length of sentences," or, in another story, "how was it, then, that she beheld the beverage in its canned form, only four bus hours' distance from home?" And: "But now he saw that the tortuosity of argumentation required to lead this character towards the first glimmers of insight would require such an expenditure of time as would altogether preclude the finding of the girl intact," thinks Mr. Durchshlag in "The Verse in the Margins."

Her streams of consciousness often read as though spoken by someone who's taught him or herself English from a dictionary, even when the characters are ostensibly speaking or thinking in their native Hebrew. They think in the second person: "There is a problem with a thing you have been given," worries the girl in "Pickled Sprouts." And constructions are often gnawingly passive, as in "the scent of baking fish isn't as awful as the raw, but when your nose suspends reports you are relieved."

When the technique works, Goldstein enmeshes you in her character's emotional state. This is particularly appropriate and effective when the narrators are children. But often it feels claustrophobic, as though we have been trapped by her characters' inarticulateness. Sometimes, the prose is simply perplexing.

While one may wish that Goldstein had strained a little less at times, her ambition and talent deserve recognition, and her work certainly deserves reading. The stories in the collection seem to fit together into a kind of episodic novel following a woman, perhaps not unlike Goldstein herself, who spends a childhood searching for a place in Israel and an adulthood seeking comfort in exile. By giving voice to those who "were never sufficiently absorbed," Goldstein has brought an age-old tradition in Jewish literature into the post-modern Zionist era.

א

MARSHALL E. WILEN *lives and writes in, though not necessarily about, New Jersey.*

Coda

Robert Pinsky

The Six-Pointed Star

The English prizefighter Daniel Mendoza was born in Whitechapel, London in 1763. He was Champion of England from 1792 to 1795. According to *The Jewish Encyclopedia*, Mendoza founded the "scientific" school of boxing. Miles's *History of British Boxing* defines the first period of pugilism as "From the Championship of Fig to the Appearance of Daniel Mendoza." "Mendoza entered the prize-ring April 17, 1787, at Barnet," says the *Encyclopedia*, "where he defeated, in less than thirty minutes, Samuel Martin, a butcher of Bath." In some instances, Mendoza defeated opponents by exhausting them so that they fell down without receiving a blow. He became sheriff's officer for the county of Middlesex in 1806. In 1820, at the age of fifty-seven, he fought his last match, being "punished" over twelve rounds by his opponent. He then retired and became a publican in Whitechapel. Mendoza was known as "The Star of Israel."

The nickname might have been different without the geometrical symbol known as the Star of David.

The six-pointed star that appears on the flag of modern Israel has been adopted by followers of Islam and by Mormons, by occultists and movie directors. A peculiar and extensively footnoted website, devoted to the subject, shows the symbol on the Mormon Assembly Hall in Salt Lake City. The authors of the site say:

> We believe that both Israel and Christians have been deceived by occultists who would have them believe that the six-pointed star is a Jewish symbol. Nothing could be further from the truth. It is not a Jewish symbol, but an occult symbol. The six-pointed star is a hexagram—a curse mark—no matter what name it may have: Star of David, Solomon's Seal, Double Triangle, Shield of David, etc. When the occult practitioner puts a curse on someone, he uses the hexagram!

The same source attributes the symbol to worship of Saturn, who is associated with greed, and points out that it appears (as the configuration of the thirteen stars above the eagle's head) on the one-dollar bill.

A friend of mine points out that this is a bit like informing Christians that since the cross is a Roman implement of torture and execution, it cannot possibly be an emblem of the truth and resurrection. The zany, earnest repulsiveness of crank iconography soars or plunges beyond mere "anti-semitism." The rigidly exclamatory definition that tries to predicate what or whose a symbol "is" violates the nature of symbols.

Here's what another website says: "This star is a symbol of the Great White Brotherhood, a collective body of both discarnate and incarnate beings from Earth and other planets and dimensions dedicated to the spiritual upliftment of all beings and is used to denote Christ Consciousness."

These voices manifest the Rorschach-test or mirror-like, multiple inspirations and imagined messages that emanate from a form. Geometrical symbols have not only different branches but different roots. The swastika used as a binding ornament on old editions of Kipling appears also in pre-Colombian decoration. Graphic designs in the imagination evolve in response to forces more various—involving events more arbitrary, tangled and enigmatic—than those that caused fish, reptile and mammal to evolve the same streamlined shape for moving through water.

Many sources interpret the linked triangles as pointing to heaven and to earth, or funnel mouths open to earth and heaven, symbolizing the intertwining of divine and secular realms. Sometimes the triangles are identified as the male "blade" and the female "chalice," making the star a Western version of the yin-yang.

As early as the reign of the Portuguese monarch Affonso iv (1325–57), who reversed earlier, benign policies, all Jews were forbidden to appear in public without wearing a visible, six-pointed yellow star on their hat or coat. In this regard the Nazis again appear as not originators but copiers, adapters, exploiters and refiners.

The first Jewish source to mention the star is in the thirteenth century of the Common Era, and the symbol does not appear to be much used before the fifteenth century, though it has been found on a much earlier Jewish tomb in Tarentum, Italy. *The Jewish Encyclopedia* says, "It is probable that it was the Kabbalah that derived the symbol from the Templars (see Vajda in 'Magyar Zsidó Szemle,' xvii. 314 et seq.; German reprint in Grunwald's 'Mitteilungen der Gesellschaft für Jüdische Volkskunde,' x. 138 et seq.)."

Although Gregory Peck wears the image on his tunic in *David and Bathsheba,* and it appears in other Biblical epics as well, the six-pointed star was not associated with King David nor with Jews, until thousands of years after the time of David. On the notorious triumphal arch of the Emperor Titus, celebrating his conquest of Palestine, the branched menorah appears, but not the anachronistic star, which does appear on the label of the sweet "Mogen David" wine served at American celebrations of Passover in the nineteen-fifties. The star is called in Arabic the "Magen Dawid."

Precisely because this geometrical figure has gone through infinite permutations of imagination and history, because it has acquired an almost endless range of meanings—demented, exotic, commercial, tragic—it may be all the more suitable as an emblem of David the son of Jesse, that many-sided poet and warrior and politician and adulterer and worshipper— whose original, and perhaps unascertainable, human depths and folds have been multiplied by the generations, from all regions and languages of the earth.

Many-sided and multiple, but not arbitrary or merely universal. David may or may not be a Moabite or the son of a slave-concubine, but he is a Jew; something similar is true of the six-pointed star, in actual modern experience. It is on the flag of Israel. It is the national symbol. It marks the graves of Jewish Americans in Normandy, and it is even more deeply Jewish, in more intricate ways, than that.

Here is a particular instance of the star, with its passions and overtones as intricately powerful as the figure of David himself: a photograph of thirteen young men, taken in the bad year 1939. Sewn onto their uniforms is the six-pointed star said to be copied from an insignia of the Templars. Their names are Ralph Binder, Joseph Siegel, Nathan Schneider, Morris Newberg, Gilbert Kaplan, Harry Silver, David Becker, Milton Silver, Milford Pinsky, Abraham Baum, and Seymour Barron. They are the Jewish Aces, in shorts, kneepads and basketball shoes. Abraham Baum is holding the ball; on it someone has painted: "City Champs, 1938–39." Milford Pinsky is holding the trophy, with its crowning figure of an athlete holding the ball high in triumph.

The group picture is an interesting artifact because of the apparently daffy or tragic incongruity of that emblem, deployed for such different purposes in Europe at the moment the photograph was taken. The players of the Jewish Aces were most likely far from unaware of the laws and measures enacted by the Third Reich. Some of them would eventually go into battle against that regime. Incongruity in the eye of the beholder? It seems safe to assume that on that sunny afternoon in Long Branch, New Jersey, beaming at the camera, they were aware of the assertive, maybe even defiant quality of the team's name: *The Jewish Aces*.

In such impure, fluid, partly inscrutable manifestations the life in history of persons and their creations makes itself known—or if not exactly known, then felt as a presence. And each stroke of time adds a new layer. In this sense, lives and creations do not exactly end, but continue as vectors of energy, durably complex particles exceeding likelihood or measure. David himself, that Jew and part-

Moabite tribal leader, poet and warrior, has, like the symbol he would not have recognized, become more Jewish, and differently Jewish, as the very idea *Jewish* has accumulated its extraordinary weight of meaning—deepening over centuries of attainment and outrage, of suffering and ordinary life, in an endless evolution and continuing, infinite accretion.

ROBERT PINSKY'S *most recent book of poems is* Jersey Rain. An Invitation to Poetry, *a Favorite Poem Project anthology, will be published this summer with an accompanying* DVD. *He was Poet Laureate of the United States 1997–2000.*

The fonts used in this book are from the Garamond family